Acclaim for **Feed the Good Dog** and Paul McCabe

There is so much in this book! I took 2 or 3 insights at a time and used them to help me look at my actions. It truly helped me.

—JIM HAYHURST, bestselling author,
The Right Mountain: Lessons from Everest

Feed the Good Dog is a direct and easy to understand guide to maximizing one's life. The book exposes the true values of life and provides the reader with a path to bring about positive results. Spend a couple of hours with a wonderful read and be part of transforming and improving your life.

—SCOTT ISDANER, President, One World Live

Feed the Good Dog is an invaluable teaching aid for life lessons and achieving personal success. We capitalized on Paul McCabe's methods and energy at Rogers Cablesystems and watched our sales on a key product jump from 50 to over 5000 per month. Now he has bundled his teaching and enthusiasm into a gem that shows how we can achieve the ultimate in success without compromising balance in our lives. Thank you, Paul, for reminding us why we get up every morning and strive to be the best that we can be. Congratulations on your new book … you are truly an inspiration!!!

—STEPHEN HAYNES, Senior V.P., MCCI Global

High achievers commit to their success and *Feed the Good Dog* is a great combination of ageless wisdom and practical insights that will help anyone in the pursuit of excellence to make that commitment. This book has power!

—VICTOR LUKE, 6th Degree Black Belt
World Taekwondo Champion

Feed the Good Dog is an inspirational and practical approach to helping individuals and corporations develop momentum towards outcomes that they want. A provocative examination of the energetic link between choices and the realization of human potential.

—PAUL MORSE, Managing Partner, Knebel Watters & Associates

Having personally trained thousands of Salespeople and Sales Managers over the last twenty years, I have some knowledge of what it takes to become a champion in life. In *Feed the Good Dog* Paul McCabe has laid out a specific route to success for anyone wanting and willing to follow his wisdom. I recommend this book as must reading for individuals with an open mind and a thirst for the better life.

—JOHN TOWNSON, John Townson & Associates Ltd.

As someone who works to set the stage for culture change within organizations through motivational training, Paul McCabe drives it home like none other. He delivers clarity! Three years after the series of seminars, employees still stop to tell me how he changed their lives both professionally and personally. Hugely impactful and the best I've ever attended in my career.

—MARK KNAPTON, VP Call Centre Operations, Bell ExpressVu

After reading the process for self-improvement outlined in *Feed the Good Dog* I was in awe of its simplicity. This book helps "disturb the present in the service of a better future." If an improved quality of life for yourself, loved ones and associates is a goal, then read this book. Read it more than once!

—LES WILLIAMS (Corporate Gardener)

Paul McCabe is responsible for single handedly changing my entire future. And to a bright one at that. With two words Paul took me from a lifer to the president of my own company. The two words… "decide to"! *Feed the Good Dog* will help anyone who graces its pages.   —JOHN LEONARD, President, Fit 4 Real

We have had the good fortune of having Paul McCabe address two of our international conferences. He is truly a dynamic speaker! Now *Feed the Good Dog* carries his knowledge and enthusiasm from presentation to print!
—KEITH BRAY, President, ASMC International

Having witnessed Paul McCabe present the material in *Feed the Good Dog,* I can offer testimony to the incredible impact he has on session attendees. The philosophy is tied in to a program that provides instant, positive and measurable results.
—JOHN GORMAN, President, John Franklin Associates

Thank you for "lighting the fire."
—CHRIS BARBEAU, Bell Canada

WOW!!! What a way to finish off an excellent seminar. You come through with the knockout punch. That was it, I was down for the count, nothing left. Thank you for three of the most intense, informative and emotional days of my life!
—DAVE WILLIAMS, SCHAWK Canada Inc.

Your seminar will be a guiding force for me to follow over the upcoming years. You were not just delivering it, you were living it!   —BRENT COWAL, Baker Gurney & McLaren

Your dynamic program will help me to build relationships and expand my book of business. Thank you for making it informative, practical, impactful and FUN!

—PRISCILLA LOW, CIM, FCSI, Nesbitt Burns

Thank you for the best seminar I have had the privilege of taking part in. Your dynamic delivery and use of real life experience highlighted the need to make a choice to succeed.

—MICHAEL DAVIES, TELUS Communications Inc.

Your program was the most comprehensive, professional approach to sales (and human relations) training I have yet to experience.

—CHET MCHENRY, John Deere

The Paul McCabe seminar I attended with my associates was the most outstanding sales seminar I have ever participated in.

—JENNY KASUBA, Manpower

Terri
Keep aiming high!

FEED THE GOOD DOG

Making the Choice to Succeed

Paul McCabe

ROSE LINE
PUBLISHING

National Library of Canada Cataloguing in Publication

McCabe, Paul
Feed the good dog: making the choice to succeed

ISBN 0-9734897-0-7

1. Self-help 2. Business

Rose Line Publishing
147 Briarwood Road
Unionville
Ontario L3R 2X1

pmccabe@comperstrat.com

Text design: Heidy Lawrance Associates

Cover design: Underfoot Communications Inc.

Printed and bound in Canada

01 02 03 04 05 06 6 5 4 3 2 1

To my beautiful daughters
Jessica and Kelly

With all of a grateful father's love

Acknowledgements

Without the involvement of Amanda O'Donovan, this book would never have seen the light of day. She not only helped with most of the support material but provided shape and structure to my "stream of consciousness" approach in our many discussions.

I have tried to incorporate the suggestions of those who have reviewed the manuscript at various stages in its evolution and sincerely thank them for their help along the way; most notably, Elaine Day, Claudia McCabe, Peter Warne, Paul Morse, David Aleksis, Jim Harris, Keith Bray, John Gorman, Bob Proctor, Gerry Robert and Sean O'Donovan.

I would also like to acknowledge my mother, Jean, for the positive affect she continues to have, for her belief in me from the outset, for her positive attitude and continued support, and for the examples she has set throughout my life.

As we are all products of our environment and each experience moulds our thoughts and actions, I am also grateful for the insights and input gained in working with the thousands of professionals who have attended my seminars and workshops. They have all contributed through the sharing of their experiences, in helping me try to keep things straight forward and realistic.

Lastly, but perhaps above all, I want to thank my wife Debbie for her constant support, encouragement, and most of all, for her love.

A Native American elder once described
his own inner struggles:
*"Inside of me there are two dogs. One of the
dogs is bad and negative. The other dog is good
and positive. The bad dog fights
the good dog all the time."*
When asked which dog wins, he reflected
for a moment and replied,
"The one I feed the most."

Foreword

Feed The Good Dog is a treasure chest of wisdom. It is born out of experience, and brought to us by someone who not only lives what he teaches but knows how to communicate deep and practical concepts in such a way that they become invaluable to anyone who is really *willing* to make the choice to succeed.

Over the years I have read countless self-improvement books, by new authors as well as celebrities. I have learned that books can transform lives. I know what a book can do for poor self-esteem, or for a struggling family. I know what the right book can accomplish for someone who is in the wrong job. I understand how valuable a book can be to anyone with an entrepreneurial mindset. I've seen how a book can turn around a bank account and I've seen books change corporate cultures.

This might well be such a book. The genius of *Feed the Good Dog* lies in its universal wisdom. Regardless of origin, circumstance, or purpose, readers everywhere can use this book to fuel the engine of progress, success and happiness. I can see this book being used in the corporate world to motivate and encourage *passion*. I can imagine this book being tremendously helpful to the therapeutic community because it is so warm, helpful and practical; at times funny and at times serious and penetrating. I can visualize this book in the hands of a salesperson, looking for a dramatic increase in performance. I can envision network marketers using this book to fire-up entire teams. I can see this book in the hands of any organization, improving morale. I can see how a single parent could use *Feed The Good Dog* to help achieve balance, or why a couple should read this book together, for mutual improvement. Personally, I can see how my teenagers will benefit from this book, as a guide through the turbulent years leading to adult life. Very few books have such diverse potential.

In reading this book, I asked myself what makes it so good? The answer lies in the mind of the personality behind *Feed The Good Dog*. Paul McCabe simply lives the book. Its pages describe his own life and his own thinking. His journey, one quickly gathers, has been extensive. Everything about this book suggests that he derives his wisdom from personal experience. He knows what he's talking about. I guess that's why Paul is such a charismatic and impactful motivator. His corporate experience shines through, as do the challenges he has faced throughout his life. It's brilliant!

What you will find in *Feed the Good Dog* is a roadmap and a game plan. For those of you who are ready, I can't think of a clearer, more touching, insightful and practical book to put you on the path to greater success. As the subtitle reveals, it's about a "choice." Read this book and it will help provide the tools you need to make the choices that will lead to the success you desire.

Read it, study it, do it, live it and then pass it along.

An awesome book!

—Gerry Robert,
Best-selling author
The Millionaire Mindset

Contents

The pose you strike, the posture you assume, the perspective you choose, the opinions you express, the behaviour you model, and the temperament you display, all speak about the person you are. You get out of life exactly what you are prepared to invest in it. Energy and enthusiasm are contagious. Attitude is everything.

Define Your Vision   38

When you feel that you have a reasonable understanding
of where you are now, you can define where it is you want
to go next, and start to create the map that's going to get
you there. Identify your assets and your liabilities and set
some goals.

Have Confidence In Yourself   62

Encourage yourself to overcome your fear of failure, tell
yourself that you're fully prepared to fail as many times as it
takes to succeed, and you'll find that you stop worrying
about what people think. Force yourself to take some risks.

Recognize Your Responsibility   88

Progress wants to happen. We've each been given something to add to this world that wasn't here before we
arrived and it's time to answer the call. Embrace change,
become accountable for your future and you'll start making
progress. Remember, the simple difference between dreams
and reality is action.

Deal With Difficulties   116

En route to success, you're going to face a series of obstacles. Don't try to walk round them. Face up to whatever is in your way, clear the path and continue with the journey. Prioritize your problems, hold on tight to your objective, and seek out people who can help you live your dream

Become A Progressive Leader   142

Like anything else, leadership can be learned. But people don't like to be led, so learn to serve. Winning coach and motivator, Lou Holtz, was so right when he suggested that everything in life and everything in business is about helping other people get what they want.

Pay It Forward 166

Sometimes, the journey itself can be more significant and enlightening than the final destination. Master the simple art of saying thank you and learn to turn your gratitude into a legacy.

The Last Words 184

7 Steps to Success 188

Sources of Influence 190

Notes 192

The First Words

Sharing the Journey

This book is as much for me as it is for you. Almost a decade ago, I made a decision to be a winner, instead of a *lifer*. I didn't want to be the kind of person who spends a lifetime with no spring in my step, no sparkle in my eye, and no vision of where I was going. I had come across too many people (myself included) who had become complacent and lacking in motivation. People who seemed to be waiting for themselves to show up. Rather than spending each day resigned to repeat the pattern of the previous one, I resolved, wherever possible, to embrace its novelty and inject my life with energy, effort and enthusiasm. I have profoundly enjoyed the journey (good and bad) that has brought me to the place I inhabit today, and I believe that I am a very different person now than the one I was all those years ago. Mine was not an overnight transformation, but rather an incremental progression, which included a lot of soul searching, mentoring, experiments and mistakes before I met with success. My refusal to remain a *lifer* has led me to identify 7 strategies or steps that I consider critical to the pursuit of success. I revisit these strategies frequently to remind myself of the common sense they contain, because I know that I don't consistently practice what I preach. In choosing to succeed, we take the most important step of our life. I know I did. But it's one thing to know what you should do, quite another to choose to do it. In this book, I'd like to review some of the key approaches I have tried to make a conscious effort to apply (not always successfully) and make those choices once more, with you.

My hope is that you'll find something between these covers that will make a significant difference to you and to the people you come into contact with every day of your life. Stressed by everyday pressures, so many of us no longer have the energy to use common sense. We are less inclined to apply ourselves to, let alone be conscious of, the reality of the moment and the importance of celebrating it. When you choose to absorb and apply some of the time-tested principles that appear within this book, then you're making a positive choice to succeed. Whether you apply them to your personal relationships, your parenting, your career, your spirituality or any other corner of your life is entirely up to you.

My intention is to engage, provoke, stimulate, even irritate into action. As you read these pages, my hope would be that you take the time to use this book to reflect on who you are and where you're going. I'd like to think that the book's content will help you to *make the choice* to bring about a measurable improvement in your quality of life, aiding you to achieve personal, professional and organizational turnaround. I'm hoping that it will fill the common gap between dreams and reality with a good call to action. Whether you consider yourself a novice, or to be at the pinnacle of achievement, you have it in you to accomplish more. If, in reading the words contained in this book, you experience even the smallest personal moment of clarity, then I've more than achieved what I set out to do.

Where's the Motivation?

The get-rich-quick deals that appear daily on our computers in the form of junk e-mail, promise us instant success in a mouse click. These are best reserved for idle dreamers. But you're not just a dreamer or you wouldn't be holding this book. You're a doer, because you're prepared to make the necessary effort to translate your dreams into action. You're willing to take a brief pause from the insanity of our overscheduled lives, to examine what it will take to live a more fulfilling existence. We all have dreams. We must have dreams. Imagination fuels creativity, which in turn enables us to exit the confines of our conditioning to explore new and rewarding territory. But if we fail to make the effort that's necessary to turn our dreams into reality, we're simply, and at best, hopeless romantics, ignoring the *responsibility* we have to fulfill every last ounce of our potential.

In the course of my work, I've come across too many people who seem to have made the choice *not* to succeed. And that seems such a waste. An individual aversion to success may lead to the disappointment of an unfulfilled life. Collectively, such an attitude can destroy the dreams and the legacy of a generation. I see a lot of people who don't make the choice. At the same time, I realize that I constantly need to remind *myself* of the importance of the choices *I'm* making, as well as the importance of how *I* react and proact.

My motivation for creating this book? You could say that I was motivated by mediocrity. We live in a time that seems obsessed with reducing everything to its lowest common denominator. Step off a plane in any major world capital and you're likely to be confronted with advertisements for the same stage shows, movies, dining experiences, fashion, art and music. Instead of taking things to the next level, we've stopped several floors short and have resigned ourselves to making do with a lacklustre package designed to suit enough of the people most of the time. We seem to have arrived at a point where we don't even care about apathy anymore!

What's Our Legacy?

Step back for a moment and examine our society. We're united by celebrity culture, instant gratification and short attention spans. We're encouraged to dream of overnight success and most of us are hungry for it, but we consistently resign ourselves to considerably less than best. However we measure it, success usually looks like someone else. We believe that success is an accident of birth, or the random outcome of fate. So, it's luck that leads someone else to write a bestseller, enjoy stardom, build a new business or make millions. The strange thing is that, while we're all hungry for success in life, and we believe that we have a right to succeed, we just don't expect to. Most of us are happy to sit around pretending that we're OK without it. Worldwide, we seem to be waiting for ourselves to show up, passively hoping for a series of lucky breaks, pretending to ourselves that success is hiding around the next corner, waiting to present us with our pre-packaged future.

Is that what we're willing to accept? The good news is that success truly *is* around the next corner, but *it's* waiting for *us* to show up. We have to choose to make the turn. If we want to win the lottery, we have to buy a ticket. I've put this book together because it's time to get up and do something. Deep down, we're all hungry for success. If you accept only this, accept the reality of that continuous *success-hunger*. People who succeed do so because they know that progress wants to happen. They've stopped pretending that everything's OK and they're hungry for a new world. Successful people make the choice to succeed; it's as simple as that.

We've got to stop listening to all the dream busting reasons why something can't be done. We've got to stop making lists of all the ideas we'd act on, if only we had the time. We've got to stop *just* wishing. We've got to stop *just* hoping. We've got to stop *just* praying. We're all full of untapped energy, potential energy that's stored within us, just wanting to happen. It's time to stop waiting for ourselves to show up because, WE'RE HERE, IT'S NOW, and there's no better time to choose to succeed.

Clear Definitions

The society that we share enjoys dividing us into clearly defined groups of winners and losers, constantly returning to the rather simplistic analogy of good versus evil. Luckily, it's not that simple. I don't believe that we're dealing with a black and white world of success vs failure. There's a galaxy of difference between failing and being a failure. Even the biggest winners have experienced loss. And, there are a lot of people out there who just haven't learned how to win. They're not wrong. They're just not right yet! As Vince Lombardi, head coach of the Green Bay Packers said, "We never lose, we just run out of time." All we need is positive support in the form of coaching, strategies and insight to beat the clock and open up a whole new future.

The Hollywood vision of success happens overnight. People want instant results but, so often, aren't prepared to nurture the dream, let alone invest in its achievement. The real life version is far more subtle and time-consuming. Success doesn't stem from a single root, nor can it be achieved without preparation. Its origins lie in a mixture of elements that we must work to align, to act as catalysts to jump-start our respective lives:

ATTITUDE: *be sure to pick the right one*

ACCEPTANCE: *make peace with your imperfections*

CIRCUMSTANCE: *act when conditions are favourable*

COMMITMENT: *promise to stay the course*

EFFORT: *learn to be proactive*

ENERGY: *be prepared to work hard*

ENTHUSIASM: *be known for your passion*

FAITH: *believe in yourself & a higher Universal power*

OPPORTUNITY: *take up the challenge*

REALITY: *be aware of your environment*

VISION: *use your imagination*

No single element can describe your future. For example, circumstance alone cannot define you or determine the direction of your dreams. It's the choices you make that determine who you are, and who you will become. We each have it within us to create our own unique vision of success.

Who Are We?

Life itself is the sum of the choices we make. And I believe that the journey to success begins with two important choices: self-examination and a winning attitude. Before we go anywhere, we've got to take a personal inventory and get to know who we are, and why. What makes us behave the way we do? How do we respond to difficult situations and to the people we interact with most closely? It's important that we come to terms with our current reality, take the time to create our vision of success, of who we want to become and where we want to be. And we need to take a long hard look at our priorities. We've got to be prepared to put first things first, separate the urgent from the important and put time aside to set (and constantly review) the goals that will lead us to live our vision. We live a life of multiple choice. Be careful which boxes you check, because even the smallest choices combine to define the person you are.

We can make a conscious choice to change our current reality by seeking, embracing, experiencing and capitalizing on the vital elements that combine to produce success. As we make the decision to step outside our respective comfort zones, we are electing to grow through change. As we choose a personal destination and focus on the journey towards it, we are better able to define and achieve our goals. As we concentrate on understanding our strengths and the ways in which we can personally contribute to our own success, we break free from the fear of failure. And as we progress towards our goals and dreams, we learn to make every moment count by celebrating what's real, what's vibrant and **W**hat's **I**mportant **N**ow. We learn to WIN.

> *Y*ou must live in the present, launch yourself on every wave, find your eternity in each moment. Fools stand on their island opportunities and look toward another land. There is no other land, there is no other life but this
>
> **HENRY DAVID THOREAU—WRITER, THINKER & NATURALIST**

My Suburban Epiphany

The day that changed my life dawned as any other, but by the time the sun had set I had met with a matchless moment of clarity that was to set me running at full throttle down a new path. It wasn't a Hollywood moment. In fact the location couldn't have been more ordinary. It wasn't scripted, directed or produced by anyone else (although a cast of thousands had doubtless contributed towards bringing me to this moment). My only companion at the instant the light went on was my dear dog, Barkley, the best therapist a man could ever hope for (really!).

My personal epiphany occurred in a neighbourhood park, just steps away from my front door, in a suburban landscape that could belong almost anywhere in the northern hemisphere. I'd reached a point in my life where I had acquired (although not necessarily earned) all the things I'd been aiming for. I'd leaped up the corporate ladder and was enjoying the rewards of a successful career. I had the nice house, the nice cars, the nice vacations and a great group of friends to share time with. Happily, I was married to a wonderfully talented woman, who had recently given birth to our first beautiful daughter. Despite all of this, I was having a hard time looking at myself in the mirror. I wasn't living up to the image I had of who a friend, a husband, a father and an employee should be.

There was something missing. And I was increasingly turning to lesser pursuits (like alcohol) to fill the void. At some level, I knew I was a man just going through the motions. True to my generation, I'd spent most of my life with an, 'I'm OK, you're OK' kind of attitude, but suddenly I realized that I wasn't OK and that I was going to have to do something about it. I caught a glimpse of myself retiring at 65, but feared that I'd probably buried myself somewhere around the age of 25, and here I was, just marking time in the intervening years.

It was at that precise moment, standing in a park in the burbs, that I decided to become *accountable*. Responsible for my addictive behaviour. Accepting of the fact that life's hard and that things go wrong. Liable for my own happiness and the happiness of those who surround me. I'm a firm believer that nothing happens by coincidence. When the student is ready, the teacher will come, and I really began to listen to, and hear, some of the central messages that surround all of us; messages that are articulated by some of the world's best motivational speakers, whose approaches resonate because they're true.

As a result of that single moment of clarity in the park I have been able to define a world in which the more I put in, and the more I participate, the more I get in return. And that makes me happy. Nowadays, when I meet obstacles, or things just don't turn out quite the way I'd planned them, I have a better understanding of the part I've played in the outcome. I'm no longer the victim of my own circumstances. Following my suburban epiphany, I sought help for my addictive behaviour, quit my job and set up my own company. I now spend my time pursuing my passion, motivating others to achieve their full potential, and earning a living in the process!

I don't pretend for a moment to be a remarkable man. I haven't invented anything extraordinary. I haven't cured a disease or engineered a plan for peace. I'm not a freshly minted multi-billionaire who originally washed up on these shores without a penny to his name. I haven't emerged triumphantly from a disadvantaged or abusive childhood. While rags-to-riches stories are often inspirational, and disadvantage frequently fuels the hunger for achievement, success doesn't have to stem from deprivation. Nor does success have to be measured in extreme terms. The wealth we are seeking may not be measured in the language of finance. We're not all aiming at the kind of absolute success we identify with someone like Bill Gates. But that doesn't prevent us from shooting at a realistic, rewarding and achievable target. Everyone has the right, the means, and the *responsibility*, to succeed on their own terms. Out in the *emotional suburbs*, there are millions of us who have the potential to make more of what we've got. We all have within us the means to turn the ordinary into the extraordinary. What we do achieve may not always be perfect, since absolute perfection may not exist. But progress does. And, after all, that's what's important, because we're here to make progress.

All truth passes through three stages. First, it is ridiculed. Then it is opposed violently. Third, it is accepted as being self-evident

ARTHUR SCHOPENHAUER—PHILOSOPHER

Hasn't This Been Done Before?

Albert Einstein once said that the secret to creativity is knowing how to hide your sources. Correspondingly, I'd be the first to admit that there may not be an original thought in this book. I cannot take credit for all of the suggestions that follow, because most, if not all have their origins in timeless universal truths. You'll find thoughts throughout these pages that transcend cultural and historical divides, and you'll recognize beliefs that share common ground in the major religions of the world. From Socrates to Anthony Robbins, the message is largely the same, although you may notice some subtle differences in the delivery! The reason for the repetition is that we tend to ignore, or at best trivialize, the message. We don't seem to be absorbing it. Generation after generation, we reject the wisdom of our predecessors, determined to follow our own path of destruction, until we (hopefully) mature into our own moments of clarity and realize that our elders might actually have been talking some sense. Sometimes that moment of clarity comes too late. I'm hoping to help you accelerate the process.

The problem with universal truths is that they become stale over time and often lose their impact. Hopefully, the words and approaches herein will help find the language to express these timeless principles in a way that relates to who you are and how you live now. More than ever, we are hungry to understand our purpose. You can use this book to provide you with the food you need to address your appetite for enlightenment.

There have been many people, places and circumstances that have influenced my own development as a motivational trainer and that have led me to the thoughts that have come together in the form of this book. Some of the people you will know through their own books, motivational speeches and inspirational videos. Others have a less public profile but have been, and continue to be, shining examples of encouragement to me. I never cease to be amazed at their capacity to do the right thing at every turn in their lives. I've made mention of many of these people in the acknowledgements, in the chapters that follow, and in the section at the back of this book that I've reserved for sources of influence. I encourage you to make good use of these references for further study of any subjects that float your particular boat.

Making the Most of This Book

Designer ski-wear won't teach you how to ski. While it may temporarily convey an aura of competence, you'd be far better advised to take lessons from an experienced instructor. And, having absorbed the advice of an expert coach, there is absolutely no substitute for practice. It is one thing to acquire the knowledge, quite another to choose to use it. I am hoping that this book will supply you with the motivation, as well as the knowledge you need, to make your own choice to succeed.

I think that things are always more easy to swallow when they come in bite-sized chunks. That's why I've tried to slice up what I'm saying into easily digestible sections of information. You'll find seven core ideas in the following chapters, each representing a choice you can make, a step you can take, or a strategy you can apply to transform your life and take it to the next extraordinary level. Why 7 steps? Well, it makes sense, because the conscious human mind holds about seven things at once. Let's not overburden ourselves with more than we were designed to absorb. The past decade has had a profound effect on the direction my life has taken, and I'd like to reflect that in each of the 7 strategies I summarize within these pages.

At the end of every section, I've included a summary of abbreviated points that were discussed in the chapter. Pause awhile to go back over what you've read, and figure out how it applies to your circumstances, your dreams and your opportunities, as well as how it resonates within you. There's nothing wrong with repetition. Repetition helps clarify and reinforce. That's how we learn. After you've paused, carry the summary with you as you embark on the next chapter. And, as you make your way through my collection of thoughts, take notes, turn over page corners, underline, highlight, or tear out whole sections; whatever works for you.

The more you are willing to apply yourself to the principles you are about to explore, the better you'll be able to measure your progress. Celebrate this commitment!

1

Begin With
an Attitude of Mind

"We either make ourselves miserable,
or we make ourselves strong.
The amount of work is the same."
CARLOS CASTANEDA, MYSTICAL PRACTITIONER

You Reap What You Sow

Love them or hate them, clichés endure for a reason. If you learned most of yours from the lips of a previous generation, chances are that, to some degree, you chose to ignore them. Meanwhile, you may have become a parent yourself, in which case you're now thoroughly convinced of the astounding wisdom encased in every cliché you pass on to your own offspring. Slowly, you too have come to the realization that these clichés have a habit of pointing us squarely in the direction of universal truths. While many of these insights have held up as true through countless generations, we still struggle to learn the lessons contained within them. As we know, history has a habit of repeating itself.

If you asked me to pick my favourite cliché, it would have to be this beautifully simple statement that contains within it so much wisdom:

"A man reaps what he sows." The passage goes on to suggest,

> *The one who sows to please his sinful nature, from that nature will reap destruction; the one who sows to please the spirit, from the spirit will reap eternal life*
>
> **GALATIANS 6:7-8**

There isn't a single one of us who hasn't harvested either the positive or negative effects of a simple choice of behaviour. The psychiatrist, Karl Menninger once said that, "Attitudes are more important than facts." I strongly believe that the most important choice you will make in your search for a successful life is attitudinal. A positive attitude is what separates the winners from the *lifers*. Unless you're prepared to take a long, hard, honest look at the current state of your mind, you might want to reconsider reading this book. If you're unwilling to indulge in a degree of self-examination, and take the necessary steps to optimize your attitude, the advice contained within these pages is likely to fall on stony ground. As any gardener will tell you, the best outdoor spaces need nurturing. It's what you put into the soil that determines what you get out of it. Life is no different. The way other people see you is a reflection of the way you think. Unless most of what goes on inside your head is positive, the crops you harvest won't look like the picture on the seed package.

Napoleon Hill believed that "All happiness and success starts in the mind." Take a moment to examine what's in yours. The pose you strike, the posture you assume, the perspective you choose, the opinions you express, the behaviour you model, and the temperament you display, all speak volumes about the person you are. You get out of life exactly what you are prepared to invest in it. Energy and enthusiasm are contagious. Attitude is everything.

They've got us surrounded again, the poor bastards

GEN. CREIGHTON W. ABRAMS JR

—US ARMY (DURING THE BATTLE OF THE BULGE)

Making Positive Choices

We live in a society that gives us the undeniable gift of political and economic freedom to pursue our dreams. We have the power to choose our own destiny. Given such an advantageous kick-off, living within the comfort of a culture that reeks of abundance, why do so many of us choose to adopt such a negative attitude to our circumstances? Why are we making ourselves, and each other, so miserable?

There is a strong disposition in youth, from which some individuals never escape, to suppose that everyone else is having a more enjoyable time than we are ourselves

ANTHONY POWELL—AUTHOR

Although the responsibility to succeed ultimately lies with the individual, success isn't all about self. It's also about how you deal with other people. Possibly the single most important decision that we make every day is how to communicate with others. The choices we make will have a significant impact on the degree of success we achieve. From the words we choose, the tone we use, the energy we inject, the expressions we wear, to the body language we adopt—everything says something profound about the way we feel about others. The kind of attitude you project to the people around you will also express how you feel about yourself, and how you communicate with yourself. Every day, whatever it is that you do, you can make a positive choice to have fun, to be creative, to be productive, and to be passionate. People respond to people with passion. The energy and enthusiasm you create as a result will spread to others, who will, in turn, pass it forward. Before you know it, you'll be surrounded by enthusiasts.

Because you're unlikely to be able to achieve anything really great entirely on your own, the quickest route to success actually starts by helping others get what they want. If you project a positive attitude and you're willing to make a difference in someone else's life, the chances are that you're going to not only share in the rewards, but those you've helped, in turn, will be encouraged to help you achieve your goals. Hook up with those who have a common vision and surround yourself with people who display an infectiously positive attitude. Most people quickly absorb the trademark qualities of the people they associate with. Choose to keep company with those you admire and respect. Seek out those who are in the process of blossoming, people who've got something to teach you, and you will find yourself growing through osmosis. Negativity breeds negativity. Avoid it, or you'll find yourself knee deep in it.

*D*on't judge each day by the harvest you reap, but by the seeds you plant

ROBERT LOUIS STEVENSON—NOVELIST, POET & ESSAYIST

Does Anyone Give A Flying Fish?

One of the most astounding examples of positive attitude that I've ever come across can be found in Seattle, Washington. If you ever find yourself in that part of the world, make sure you visit Pike Place Market and take yourself to the Pike Place Fish stand. It's not the only purveyor of fish in the marketplace, and it's not very big, but it's impossible to miss. Why? Well, for a start, whatever time of day you visit, Pike Place Fish is buzzing. You'll notice that the fishmongers who work there aren't standing behind the counter serving. Most of them are out in the thick of things, talking, working the large crowd, getting involved. The energy is electric, the fish are literally flying through the air and the people in the crowd are dying to get in on the action. These guys, who are constantly interacting with each other and with their customers, have turned the simple act of selling fish into a performing art. The fishmongers are buzzing and so are the people who have come to see them! The most amazing thing about it all is that this isn't an occasional performance, staged for the benefit of an audience at random points throughout the day. This is the way the Pike Place fishmongers do business, year round.

A colleague of mine, Peter Giroux, had been so impressed by a training video about Pike Place Fish, that he decided to visit the Farmer's Market in Seattle and see for himself. He couldn't believe that the energy he saw on the video could be real and sustained. He visited the fish stand at 7:00 A.M., then again at 1:00 P.M. He came back for more at 4:00 P.M. and then finally at 6:30 P.M. He was amazed that the positive energy of these guys was the same on all four occasions. They were still mingling, getting involved, throwing fish, 'breaking down barriers' and transferring their energy to their customers. Throughout the day, there's a consistent group of around 60 people crowding the fish stand. At 4:00 P.M., despite the large crowds, Jason, fish catcher extraordinaire, spotted my colleague and recognized that he'd already been to the market twice that same day. Out of the hundreds of faces he sees every day, Jason is still able to focus on the individual and recognizes the importance of doing so. In doing so, he maximizes his relationships with all of his customers.

Would you be happy selling fish? I've never done it myself, but I can't imagine it's the most inspiring of professions. To start with, while the rest of us are still snugly tucked up in bed, you'd be up with the birds to welcome the day's catch. And, while most of the country is hitting the snooze button, you'd already be elbow deep in chunks of ice, attempting to create an attractive display of dead fish. You'd then spend the day on your feet, talking about the price of fish, and most of the evening trying to get the smell of it out of your clothes. Doesn't sound like a very attractive way of spending your days, does it? Well, that all depends on your attitude.

Love What You Do

When John Yokoyama bought the unassuming little fish stand known as Pike Place Fish, he was having trouble making his car payments. A decade later he faced bankruptcy. Today he's a corporate cult figure, heading up an organization that is now known to thousands of people worldwide. Although he still sells plenty of it, fish is no longer his only focus. Fish, for John Yokoyama, and many who share his vision, has become a management philosophy. John is now a highly paid keynote motivational speaker, who tours worldwide with his Flying Fish consulting team, which includes his fellow fishmongers. To date, his business culture has spawned 2 books, 3 videos, endless TV coverage and a whole collection of fishy merchandise.

What prompted the transformation? Yokoyama had spent his early childhood in a US internment camp for Japanese Americans during World War II. He confesses to being an "angry young man," who drove people away. His management style at Pike Place used to be command and control, bordering on the tyrannical. However, a series of personal growth seminars in the nineties helped him address his anger and he began changing the way he interacted with his employees.[1] John learned how to empower his team of fishmongers. And they transformed the everyday routine of running a market fish stand into an infectiously playful, creative and energetic world of flying fish. It was a new world that challenged customers to join in and become an integral part of the whole theatrical experience. Together these fishmongers discovered how to live for the moment. They learned to love what they do, even when they weren't exactly doing what they loved.

Rules of Engagement

I've personally had enough negative retail experiences throughout my life to send me rushing into the arms of anyone who acts as though they're hungry for my business. Over the years, I've lost count of the number of times I've had to wait for an assistant to finish a personal conversation before bothering to find out why I'm standing waiting on the other side of the counter. I'm tired of walking into stores that are staffed by people who make it clear they'd rather be elsewhere, and who constantly pass the buck. I try to avoid places where people can't be bothered to take initiative, because, unless my request fits the mould, I'll never come away satisfied. The reason that Pike Place Fish Market has become such a success is that the people who work there make the choice to embrace the rules of engagement, finding the collective energy and commitment to become proactive, imaginative, attentive, engaging and *accountable*.

The very first step they took involved a fundamental shift in attitude. They each made the decision, whatever their personal circumstances, to come to work every day ready to have fun and to remain entirely focused in the moment. These fishmongers were willing to make the simple choice to be happy. It's not rocket science, but so many of us find it so very hard to achieve. The Pike Place Fish employees decided to break down the traditional barriers between vendors and customers. These guys started to walk out in front of the fish display and actively engage their customers, as if they were an audience. They even went so far as using the fish as props (think jumping monkfish). Not everybody bought fish. Some just came to watch the show, but that didn't matter, because every casual passerby was a potential customer. Build up a rapport with someone and they might be back tomorrow with money in their pockets.

When a customer picks out a fish, instead of walking back behind the counter to weigh, price and package, the Pike Place people have found that it is more fun to throw the fish to a colleague behind the counter. The spectacle of flying fish has become so popular that customers get drawn into the excitement and are often invited to have a go at fish throwing themselves. That's guaranteed to make someone's day. And, as the fish are flying, there'll be a constant dialogue going on between the fishmongers and their customers. Details of a purchase are given a humorous twist, repeated by the team members at the top of their voices, and then linked in some way to the customer, who temporarily becomes the star of the show. Pike Place Fish has become known for always being prepared to do whatever it takes to deliver excellent customer service.

There are three other fish stands in the Pike Place Market, and their fish is generally cheaper, but none of them draws the crowds like the Pike Place Fish Co.

Define Your Attitude

How would you describe your own attitude? If this is a challenge, or in fact a struggle, I'm going to suggest that you learn how. Start by asking yourself the classic question. Is your glass half empty or half full? Do you think in terms of abundance, or scarcity? Be honest with yourself, how do you tend to react to what life throws at you? Do you always feel like you've drawn the short straw, that you've been unfairly treated, that everyone else is having a more enjoyable life than yours? Or do you bounce, spring-loaded into every new day, ready to make that glass overflow? These may be extreme examples and I use them simply to illustrate a point. Most of us inhabit the middle ground. Even so, before you can start working on your new attitude, it's very important to understand what kind of attitude you already have.

> *What lies behind us and what lies before us are tiny matters compared to what lies within us*
>
> RALPH WALDO EMERSON—AUTHOR, POET & PHILOSOPHER

Would you consider yourself a reactive or a proactive person? Do you take initiative, or are you more likely to follow in the footsteps of others? Do you consider yourself to be a victim of circumstance and do you often find yourself blaming others for the situations you're in, or do you choose to take full responsibility for your actions and recognize the part you play in the outcome of all your encounters? Do you shoot from the hip when other people blindside you with their behaviour, or do you prefer to count to ten and weigh your response before wading in? Do you take initiative, make your own choices and hold yourself accountable for them, or do you find yourself adapting to a course that others have set for you?

If, after careful consideration, you find yourself weighing in with more of a reactive personality, don't worry, all is not lost! The way we deal with life results from a multitude of influences that have brought each of us to the current stage of our respective careers as human beings, (but more on that later). What's important now, is that you recognize your mindset and understand that there's plenty you can do to alter it. Norman Vincent Peale told us that self-correction begins with self-knowledge. Inside every reactive person there's an alter ego just dying to assume a leadership role. And, in case you need further convincing, the number 1 Habit on Stephen R. Covey's famous list of 7 recommends a proactive approach to life:

> *B*eing proactive is more than taking initiative. It is accepting responsibility for our own behavior (past, present and future) and making choices based on principles and values rather than on moods or circumstances. Proactive people are agents of change and choose not to be victims, to be reactive, or to blame others. They do this by developing and using four unique human gifts— self-awareness, conscience, imagination, and independent will—and by taking an inside-out approach to creating change. They resolve to be the creative force in their own lives, which is the most fundamental decision anyone ever makes

STEPHEN R. COVEY—CONSULTANT, EDUCATOR & AUTHOR

What do you say when you talk to yourself? Just because no one can hear those conversations that go on inside your head, doesn't mean that they have no effect. The more you fill your head with negative thoughts, the more your behaviour will be a predictor of bad outcomes. As Earl Nightingale, an inspirational pioneer of the self-improvement movement, said, "You become what you think about", an echo of the words Marcus Aurelius used hundreds of years before, when he declared, "A man's life is what his thoughts make of it."

Acclaimed psychologist and pioneer of Positive Self-Talk, Dr. Shad Helmstetter, tells us that, "…the subconscious mind is a sponge. It will believe anything you tell it—it will even believe a lie—if you tell it often enough and strongly enough. The brain makes no moral judgments, it simply accepts what you tell it."[2]

Helmstetter reminds us that so much of what we are thinking every day is negative. This can also be true of our conversations. How many times have we caught ourselves sitting down with friends and complaining about our problems, instead of celebrating our opportunities? These negative thoughts and conversations allure us into becoming complacent and satisfied with mediocrity. Our current reality is based on our beliefs about ourselves, whether true or not. If we reinforce existing negative beliefs and constantly listen to the dark and pessimistic side of our 'inner voice,' current reality quickly becomes a future reality without promise. Homeopathic and naturopathic practitioners tell us that our thoughts are far more powerful than many of us imagine. The way we think can have a profound effect on our physical well-being. We're literally capable of thinking ourselves sick.

By learning what to say when we talk to ourselves, and by turning Positive Self-Talk into a permanent habit, it is possible to optimize the 'inner voice' that lies within all of us. Just as we can make ourselves sick, our minds can also be proficient healers, if we want them to be. We each have the power to choose our own thoughts, so we only have ourselves to blame if we perpetuate negative ones. We are all talented and skilful individuals and it is time that we started telling ourselves as much. We become what we believe, which is why it is so important to believe the best for ourselves. It is our responsibility to celebrate our mission, our values, our assets and the contribution that each of us can make. By learning to live in the moment and focus on what matters now, we learn how to make affirmative progress. Equipped with a positive mindset, and a clear understanding of what lies within our sphere of control, we learn to listen hard and communicate well. By choosing to nurture positive and self-supportive thoughts, we are making the choice to succeed.

A Native American elder once described his own inner struggles: *"Inside of me there are two dogs. One of the dogs is bad and negative. The other dog is good and positive. The bad dog fights the good dog all the time."* When asked which dog wins, he reflected for a moment and replied, *"The one I feed the most"*.

In his best selling book, *The Power of Positive Thinking*, Norman Vincent Peale remarked that one of the greatest human tragedies is our tendency to spend our whole life perfecting our faults. Think how much more productive our lives would be if we could turn negative thinking into positive action.

> *Watch your thoughts; they become words*
> *Watch your words; they become actions*
> *Watch your actions; they become habits*
> *Watch your habits; they become character*
> *Watch your character; it becomes your destiny*
>
> FRANK OUTLAW—ACTOR

How often have you wished you'd responded differently? It's just about time to pack up after a long and tiring day. As you're firing off a few e-mail responses and shuffling papers into respectable piles on your desk, a colleague storms into your office. The body language says it all as he comes to a halt about an inch away from your face, eyes popping. Your hackles are already rising just reading this, aren't they? He accuses a member of *your* team of undermining *his* authority and holds *you* personally responsible. You were completely unaware of the situation until now. (If this particular example doesn't paint the picture for you, it works just as well if you substitute an angry parent at the school gates, verbally attacking your child, or a sports coach, who accuses you of bad parenting due to the behaviour of your son during last week's game). In each case, you're the one that's being attacked and held responsible for someone else's behaviour. You feel vulnerable and you see yourself as the victim; the other person is the aggressor. Many of us would feel that responding in the same manner would be appropriate. Surely we'd be well within our rights to fly off the deep end. It would give us such satisfaction to belt a scathing response right back at him. He deserves it after all, doesn't he? Sure, it would make us feel better, but next time *you're* faced with a similar situation, why not stop, take a deep breath and consider your response? Understand that when someone acts impulsively, you have the power to turn a potentially bad situation into a positively good one. Instead of picturing yourself as the victim of someone else's rage, know that your response has the power to determine the outcome. By responding sympathetically, you're likely to diffuse the situation and give both of you time to think calmly and positively. You'll be in control of the situation and the victory you enjoy will be far sweeter than the one based on revenge.

Is this really you? How many times have you found yourself acting like someone else? Faced with a group of strangers and a new situation, many of us compromise our integrity by submerging part of who we are. We're not comfortable with revealing our whole self, so we leave part of it behind, waiting for a moment when it is safe to emerge as who we really are. But, if you're going to get the best out of the people you meet throughout your life, you've got to be prepared to take a holistic approach. Every one of us plays multiple roles as employees, employers, parents, children, siblings, community members, volunteers, masters and servants. The mistake we so often make is trying to separate these roles. It just doesn't work, because they're all part of the same person. If you aren't prepared to be yourself, and bring every bit of you to every one of your encounters, it's unlikely that other people will reveal their true colours to you either. And that makes for extremely complicated relationships.

Are you listening to me? The fishmongers at Pike Place Market found that, by living in the moment, not only did they feel better about themselves, but their customers also bought more fish. They made the decision to focus all their energies on each interaction they had with a customer and to be entirely present for that person. They weren't merely going through the motions. It's an attitude that works every time. We're all flattered when we're made to feel important. The more you show that you care about someone, the more that person is likely to trust you and return your focus. And it's surprising how quickly the momentum gathers.

Have you ever found yourself talking to someone on the phone, and got the distinct impression that they're using the time to do a bit of multitasking? Perhaps they've got one eye on the TV, or they're tapping away on the keyboard, or they constantly interrupt your conversation to speak with someone else? Not good! We should all take the time to become genuine listeners, giving our undivided attention to what the other person is really saying, and making sure that we absorb and understand it. Dale Carnegie reminds us that everybody wants to feel important. One of the best ways to ensure that happens is to listen attentively, understand what's being said and, in the process, make someone feel like they're the only person that matters. Indeed, it's *our responsibility* to correctly hear what's being said.

How often do you laugh? Perhaps our attitude nowadays is altogether too serious. People don't function properly when they're unhappy. In contrast, when they're having fun, people automatically become more productive. So, why do we ration our enjoyment and limit it to certain pockets of our lives? Who's to say that we can't have fun at work? Why just equate pleasure with leisure? Having fun doesn't necessarily mean being childish. Why do we think that youth has cornered the market in enjoyment? Combine the uninhibited spontaneity of a child with the ordered world of adult intelligence and experience, and you've created a very powerful force. It's all about adopting a more creative attitude, whatever your age; opening up the imagination to new possibilities and breaking down the sober barriers that we've been building most of our lives.

What Is It About Seattle?

Do you believe in the collective power of a group of individuals? Could an attitude of mind infect an entire community? Just when we thought that the West Coast had given us its best and brightest, up pops Reggie Wilson, the singing bus driver. He's the man with the power to transform a busload of cynical, jaded and *lifer*-like commuters into a collection of singers who project the kind of uninhibited enthusiasm you'd expect from a kindergarten choir. While his passengers may board the bus as strangers, they've built meaningful bonds by the time they reach their respective stops. First-time riders are often speechless, but regulars will let other buses pass by to wait for Reggie. And everyone's smiling on Reggie's bus, because he won't let them on unless they do. His formula is simple. He makes a daily choice to project an optimistic attitude. But, more importantly, he's proactively positive, spontaneously engaging each of his customers as they board the bus and, throughout the ride, doing everything he can to make sure that his passengers interact with each other. He's even been known to hide little packets of cheese and crackers under selected seats, to encourage his riders to share an early morning snack on the way to work. Driving a bus can be a thankless job, filled with stress, time pressure and difficult customers. Reggie has succeeded in transforming a dreary bus ride into an experience his customers look forward to. And, when his passengers arrive at work, his positive attitude gets passed on to their customers. It's an attitude that seems to be infecting an entire city![3] Here's one man in a large city who makes a choice to make a difference.

Use Your Imagination

Everything that exists is created first in the imagination, and secondly in reality, through activity. Remember when you used to let your imagination run wild? Seems like a long time ago, doesn't it? For the *lifers* and the also-rans, the imperative of keeping up with a busy schedule of conflicting interests leaves little time for imaginative pursuits. What a sad reality. To quote Albert Einstein, "Imagination is more important than knowledge. Knowledge is limited. Imagination encircles the world." And that's not going to change anytime in the near future. Today's economy is becoming increasingly ideas-based. Companies deal in intellectual capital. There is now a value attached to the collective ideology that drives our societies. A person's willingness to generate ideas is becoming an increasingly important measure of success. It's the people with the ideas that are going to come out on top in the shuffle. The best ideas come from the most creative minds, and the most creative minds have imposed no limits on imagination.

The man who has no imagination has no wings
MUHAMMAD ALI—BOXER & PHILOSOPHER

Mark Twain once said that, "You can't depend on your eyes when your imagination is out of focus." And I say, "Have fun playing in your own sandbox". We must be prepared to nurture our imaginative spirit and develop the playful, open attitude of mind that brings our lives sharply into focus and accelerates the pursuit of our passions.

Join the Circus

Close your eyes for a moment and picture your boss. If you don't have one, just temporarily borrow someone else's. Hold that mental portrait, and then imagine for a moment that this authoritative figure you're seeing in your mind's eye is a fire-breathing, stilt-walking, accordion-player. Having a little difficulty bringing that one into focus? It's not exactly the image that springs to mind when you think about your boss, however much of a clown he or she might be. What if I told you that this fire breathing musician really exists, and is CEO of a multimillion dollar, international organization employing over 2 thousand people, with a list of more than 30 million customers, across 4 continents?

High-school dropout, Guy Laliberté is one of the founders and Chief Executive Officer of the world-famous Cirque du Soleil. Beyond circus, beyond theatre, beyond music, beyond dance, Cirque du Soleil has created a highly original, surreal, almost hallucinogenic form of live performance, with the aim of entertaining, uplifting and enlightening audiences around the world. Costumes seem to come from another dimension, expertly engineered to be as practical as they are unfamiliar. Acrobats weave their skills into the narrative and perform a spectacular series of stunts that minutes ago were thought to be impossible. Stage sets become climbing frames. The spectacle is as individual-istic as it is nonconformist and audacious, and about as far away from Dumbo the Elephant as you could possibly get.

> *Nurture your mind with great thoughts, for you will never go any higher than you think*
>
> **BENJAMIN DISRAELI**
> **—NOVELIST, DEBATOR, PRIME MINISTER AND DANDY**

Starting with a simple dream, a vivid imagination, and a lot of hard work, Guy Laliberté has taken the company from a small band of street performers in Baie St Paul, near Quebec City, to an international brand, encompassing a culturally diverse group of artists, starring in 8 concurrent shows, playing to an annual audience of over 7 million people. Despite the exponential growth, the integrity and humanity of the performance is still intact.

*W*e are not limited by money, but rather by the poverty of our dreams

DOUG WEAD
—PRESIDENTIAL ADVISOR

One of a growing number of organizations that no longer measure success purely in terms of the bottom line, Cirque du Soleil is using its influence to create social and cultural programs that focus on respect for the individual and his or her unique talents. Cirque du Soleil has selected Montreal as the location for its state of the art headquarters and is committed to the rejuvenation of the St. Michel neighbourhood it has chosen to call home. Not bad for a group of street performers.

Cirque du Soleil was born of an attitude of mind. The group waged war on indifference and had the audacity to reject everything that had been done before, even if it had worked. They risked everything on their first big show in L.A. If it hadn't been successful, they would have had to sell their Big Top to get home and the dream may have died. Each time they create a new performance, they break all the rules they've already established, in order to dream bigger, demand more, and create entirely new ways of thinking. After all, it would be insanity to do the same thing over and over again and expect different results. Wouldn't it?

Attitude: Run That By Me Again

- **Put together an attitude inventory**
  Who are you and how do others see you?

- **Be prepared to make corrections**
  If you don't change the CD, you'll always hear the same
  old songs

- **Recognize the link between behaviour and response**
  Happiness is your responsibility; don't blame others if
  you lack it

- **Create your own sandbox**
  Choose to have fun, be creative, learn to laugh, be playful
  & be passionate

- **Surround yourself with positive attitudes**
  Problem-thinkers will forever drag you down

- **Get the most out of every situation**
  Instead of procrastinating, try living in the moment

- **Make the first move**
  Take initiative and be engaging

- **Don't divorce yourself from your thoughts**
  The state of your mind and the state of your life are inseparable

- **Be reasonable in your responses**
  You have the power to turn negative force into positive achievement

- **Remain true to yourself**
  One of the most accurate indicators of success is integrity

- **Take the time to listen**
  Show that you understand

- **Nurture your imagination**
  It's more important than your knowledge and it will take you further

2

Define Your Vision

---

*"Without goals you become what
you were. With goals, you
become what you wish."*
JAMES FADIMAN, AUTHOR & TEACHER

Where Are You?

If you're planning a vacation trip, the destination you choose
will reflect the kind of person you are, or maybe the one you
wish to be. Will you be scaling volcanoes and riding rapids, or
lying on a sandy beach sipping a cocktail and reading a book?
Will you be making your travel arrangements personally, or will
you enlist the help of an agent? Do you like to travel independ-
ently, or do you prefer to be part of an organized group? Have
you set your sights on the other side of the globe, or would you
be more comfortable exploring a little closer to home? Are you
aiming to repeat a fondly remembered vacation memory from
childhood, or are you eager to explore unknown territory?

If you're going to get the best out of your vacation, you need to think about where you've already been, what you've already done, and where you've always dreamed of going. You need to be realistic about your expectations. It's no good booking a flight for Sydney, Australia if you've only got the funds to get you to the end of your street. You don't want to book a berth on an icebreaker if you get seasick and can't stand the cold. But, let's assume that you've spent some time thinking about your vacation, and that the booking you've made is a pragmatic one. Now you're going to need to spend some time planning how to get there and what to take with you.

Why would life be any different?

Remember that we're all here to make progress. We're not here to repeat history. We should be making our own. So, before you embark on your journey to success, take the time to look back on the voyage that you've made so far. What got you to this point? Create a mental documentary of the person you are, the people and events that have influenced you, the challenges you've faced and the successes you've achieved. Be honest with yourself about your unique strengths, weaknesses, talents, habits, passions and preferences. Take time to examine the relationships you have with people whose lives intersect yours. When you feel that you have a reasonable understanding of where you are now, you can define where it is you want to go next, and start to create the map that's going to get you there.

Producing Your Documentary

We've already talked about the importance of self-awareness, and we have taken a long, hard look at the kind of attitudes that define us. You're probably still working on your attitude. So am I, every day! The beauty of lifelong learning is that everything's a work-in-progress, and improvement is incremental. Remember, we're not aiming for perfection. Rather, we are focusing on progress. However, there's nothing wrong with multitasking, so I'd like you to take what you've already learned about yourself and turn it into something more substantial. Now's the time to develop the personal inventory of your mind into a private documentary of your life.

For this, you're going to need some quiet space. You won't be able to concentrate with the TV on, the CD player blasting and the phone ringing off the hook. Take yourself into a quiet room, apart from your everyday distractions, and lay the first part of your life out before you (and by that I mean summarize what you've done to date). You might be the type of person who takes stock of a situation visually, in which case sit down quietly in an armchair, close your eyes and imagine your life arranged neatly before you in clearly defined segments. If you prefer to see things written down, grab some paper and get scribbling, cover the wall with little notes, get busy with your white board, or put your laptop to work. There are many different ways you can go about this, each one as different as the person conducting the exercise. For simplicity's sake, I'm going to suggest a number of ways you might like to introduce some structure into the task, but feel free to adapt the methods to suit your personal preferences:

A Personal Checklist

We've all evolved sufficiently to understand that success cannot be viewed purely in financial terms. A stream of clichés comes to mind, but the one about money not buying you happiness probably has it nailed. The degree of wealth you enjoy cannot be used as the only measure of your achievement. Nor is success focused solely on your source of income. It would be limiting to evaluate yourself purely in terms of the job you do, whether it's as a CEO of a multinational corporation or as a parent bringing up a child. We're each a unique mixture of interests, influences and responsibilities, and within the balance of these, our success will be measured.

We each relate to the world in many different ways. In his best selling book, *First Things First*[4], Stephen R. Covey expresses our basic human needs in the following words, "to live, to learn, to love, to leave a legacy." I have yet to find a better way to articulate these needs. We all have physical needs that must be met in order to ensure survival. We rely on a source of income to clothe, feed, house and protect us. We count on continued good health to equip us with the strength and the energy to carry on, plus the vitality to extract the very best out of life. If we are going to progress, we have a responsibility to develop our mental capacity, by committing ourselves to a path of personal growth and learning throughout life. Our sociability, the way we relate to friends, family, and even complete strangers, reflects our profound requirement to love and to be loved. And our spiritual search to understand the reason for our existence, along with the need to live a meaningful life that contributes to the greater good, leads us to strive to leave a legacy.

Covey suggests that we are all too accustomed to using time as a means of managing our lives and measuring our success. Instead of watching a clock, he recommends using a compass and pointing it true north, because where we're going is far more important than how fast we get there. Each aspect of our life is just as important as the next. But many of us practise compartmentalization, ignoring the requirement for a more integrated approach to our fundamental needs. It is only by meeting our needs and paying equal attention to all of them that we will develop the necessary synergy to create depth and balance in our lives.

I was recently struck by the thoughts of Cheryl Richardson, author and life coach, who prepares clients to reap the benefits of more abundant lives.[5] Like Covey, she questions the idea of Time Management as the only means to a more organized life, arguing that it is impossible to produce sanity from an insane situation. When talking about creating an abundance of time, she firmly believes that less is more, " A high quality life has a lot more to do with what you remove than what you add to it." Richardson advocates self-management before time-management. By establishing clear life boundaries and self-centred goals ahead of work-centred goals, she argues that we will achieve more balanced, and more abundant lives.

As you reflect on each area of your life, divide your thinking into rows and columns. Note down, as a rough estimate, what percentage of your time you spend respectively on living, loving, learning and leaving a legacy. Keep a record of what you think you do well, and where you think there's room for improvement, in each area. Don't stop to think too long about each point. Let your feelings flow in a stream of consciousness, and don't discount anything, however trivial or embarrassing you might think it.

Assets & Liabilities

Next, consider the strengths and weaknesses that you bring to each area of your life. Enlist the help of a close friend or family member, someone who has known you for a while and who knows you well. You'll gain a clearer perspective if you're courageous enough to do it. You'll be reminded of some of the assets that you've started to take for granted, as well as some of the potential areas for growth you might have been avoiding. Whether you're keeping track of all this in your head, or on paper, your table might look something like the one on the next page.

Take a moment and try to clearly identify your weaknesses and the aspects of your life that you'd like to improve. This is a critical step in the process of becoming self-aware. It's important to understand why bad things have happened and at least as valuable to recognize how different behaviour and reactions could have produced a better outcome. But don't dwell on it. It's equally important to move on, turning your self-awareness into self-acceptance. You won't be able to change your attitude completely, nor will you be able to wipe out your weaknesses; they're part of what makes you who you are. The mistakes of

	What's Good?	What's Bad?	Strengths?	Weaknesses?
CAREER Time Spent?				
HEALTH Time Spent?				
FAMILY Time Spent?				
SOCIAL Time Spent?				
SPIRITUAL Time Spent?				
EDUCATIONAL Time Spent?				

your past will always be there. Acknowledge them, embrace them and then let go of them. Understand that the mistakes of your past don't have to define the outcome of your future. Accept the fact that you are not perfect but that you still have the right to succeed.

> *We did not change as we grew older; we just became more clearly ourselves*
>
> **LYNN HALL—AUTHOR IN 'WHERE HAVE ALL THE TIGERS GONE?'**

Back to the Future

Now, let's get down to the business of the future. Go back to your table, and create a complete list of all the positives you've written down. Make a mental note of where your assets lie, take a moment to focus on what's right about today, and remind yourself about the accomplishments that you are proud of.

Give some thought to the balance between the 6 rows on the table you've just completed. Depending on the stage of life you have reached, you're likely to be dedicating more time to certain activities than others, and that's only natural. During your prime earning years, your career interests are likely to dominate. As a young parent, family will absorb a disproportionate slice of your time. As you begin to age, keeping healthy is likely to become a greater priority. But beware of any extreme inequities. Is your life dangerously out of balance and do you need to take some fundamental corrective action? For each of the areas you've chosen to assess, take a while to concentrate on your next steps. Starting now, what is it that you're going to be doing with your career, your health, your family, your friends, your soul and your mind that will be different? What is it that you would like to change?

Setting Some Goals

Earl Nightingale believed that, "People with goals succeed because they know where they're going." Your ability to set goals and to create action plans to accomplish those goals will, to a large extent, dictate your degree of success. Some of the world's best-known motivational trainers like to use a reference that dates back to the fifties, and illustrates the enormous power of goal setting. The story goes something like this. A survey of the graduating class of 1953 at Yale University found that only 3% of the students had written goals. By 1973, those goal-setting students had accumulated more wealth than the balance of the class combined! It's also been suggested that, not to be outdone by Yale, the Harvard Business School conducted a similar study in 1984, tracking the success rate of its class of 1964. Reportedly only 5% of the 1964 class had taken the time to write down their goals. Two decades later, 95% of this small group had achieved their objectives, while only 5% of those who'd not committed their thoughts to paper reached the same level of success[6 & 7]

I would rather stumble a thousand times
   Attempting to reach a goal
Than to sit in a crowd
In my weather-proof shroud
A shriveled and self-satisfied soul
I would rather be doing and daring
All of my error filled days
Than watching, and waiting, and dying
Smug in my perfect ways
I would rather wonder and blunder
Stumbling blindly ahead
Than for safety's sake
Lest I make a mistake
Be sure, be safe, be dead

AUTHOR UNKNOWN

The Ivy-League illustrations highlight the experience of countless successful people and underline the direct link between goal-setting and ultimate success. Still, the majority of us fail to set anything resembling a goal. Why don't more people give themselves goals to aim for? I think there are four main reasons:

1. They don't understand their importance
2. They don't know how
3. They fear rejection of the goal by others
4. They fear failure

*O*ur plans miscarry because we have no aim. When
a man does not know what harbour he is making
for, no wind is the right wind

SENECA—ROMAN DRAMATIST, STOIC PHILOSOPHER & POLITICIAN

Winners set goals. *Lifers* mean to, but never quite get around to it. A goal is simply a written dream with a time limit. It has its origins in a burning desire, and it feeds itself from that fire within. The more intense the desire, the greater the likelihood of success. This burning desire will drive you forward, beyond the difficulties, beyond the disappointments and beyond the obstacles that you will encounter.

In order to be worthwhile, a goal must be:

Personal

It must be yours and you must feed it with faith and conviction

Realistic

Be perfectly honest about what you really want

Achievable

Believe that you can stretch yourself far enough to attain it

Challenging

Your probability of success should be approximately 50/50

Rewarding

It should result in a sense of accomplishment

Measurable

Define your goals in terms of output and results

Written

When you see it in print, your goal becomes a commitment

Clear, Specific, Vivid

A clear and detailed picture will keep you focused on method

Time Limited

A goal without a time limit is an illusion

Profoundly Desired

You won't reach your goal without 'a fire in the belly'

A dream is just a dream. A goal is a dream with a plan and a deadline

HARVEY MACKAY—MOTIVATIONAL BUSINESS SPEAKER

Ask Yourself Some Questions

If you're having difficulty trying to work out exactly what your goals are, or should be, try asking yourself the following questions:

1. What 5 things do I value most in life?
2. What are my 3 greatest ambitions?
3. How would I spend my time if I only had 6 months to live?
4. How would I change my life if I became an instant millionaire?
5. What have I always wanted to do and been afraid to try?
6. What activities give me the greatest pleasure, self-esteem and fulfillment?
7. What would I dream of doing if I knew I couldn't fail?

I always wanted to be somebody, but I should have been more specific

LILY TOMLIN—COMEDIAN

Ask yourself who you will be, what you will do and what you will have in your life when you reach your goals. You can do this in stages, if you like. Who will I be a year from now? What will I be doing in 5 years time? What will my life be like when I retire? It is important that you visualize what your situation will look like. We identify most closely with what we can see. I recently came across a very powerful story, of unknown origin, that underlines the importance of visualization. Major James Nesmeth used to be a weekend golfer, shooting in the mid to low nineties. After a seven-year break, and in worse physical condition than before, the Major came back to the game, to hit an amazing 74. How did he do it? By spending 7 long years imagining exactly what his game would look like. During that time, James had been a prisoner of war in North Vietnam, confined to a cage that was approximately four and a half feet high and five feet long. He saw nobody, spoke to nobody and had no physical exercise. To occupy his mind, he learned to visualize. Every day he played 18 holes on his favourite golf course. He imagined the clothes he was wearing, the changing weather conditions, the smell of the grass, the sand traps, the water hazards and the soft clunk of the ball as it made it to the hole. He concentrated on his grip, his swing and his follow through and carefully tracked the progress of his ball each time he made a shot. He had plenty of time on his hands to perfect each shot and sink every putt. It was as if he had played golf every day for 7 years. And he improved his game by 20 strokes.[8]

Jack Nicklaus acknowledges a similar imaging technique, "I never hit a shot even in practice without having a sharp in-focus picture of it in my head. It's like a color movie. First I 'see' the ball where I want it to finish—nice and white and sitting up high on the bright green grass. Then the scene quickly changes, and I 'see' the ball going there; its path, trajectory and shape, even its behavior on the landing. Then, there's sort of a fade-out, and the next scene shows me making the kind of swing that will turn the previous images into reality. Only at the end of this short private Hollywood spectacular do I select a club and step up to the ball."[9] Mental imaging is a technique used widely by successful sportsmen and women. It also worked well for Walt Disney. On Saturdays, he would take his daughters to a local park to ride the carousel. While he sat and watched his girls enjoying themselves, he would imagine an elaborate park, filled with families, and containing all the characters he'd created. With no preceding model to work with, he created the blueprint for a whole new world of family entertainment.[10] Practise using the same technique for any of your own dreams. Unless you can see yourself shooting par or better, you're unlikely even to make the green.

When Will Your Dreams Come True?

Pay close attention also to the timing of your goals. Are you investing all your hopes and ambitions in retirement? Of course, there are certain life imperatives that may prevent you from realizing particular dreams before you have the leisure time to address them. If you have dependents who rely on you as a source of income, it may be impractical to take a year off to backpack around the world. But make sure you aren't putting off living the life you really want until the day that retirement dawns. You may find you're too old to sleep in a tent.

*I*t seemed to me that the idea of retirement we were
   taught means that you work to pay bills for the bulk
of your life, while postponing all the things you truly
want to do until your winter years. I didn't want to do
that, and I don't believe anyone else does either

ASHA TYSON—HOMELESS AT 17, RETIRED AT 26!

Asha Tyson, who was neglected and abused as a child,
homeless at 17 and retired at 26, believes that we have been
duped by our compartmentalized lives into thinking that
retirement comes during the last portion of our time on earth.
In her book, *How I Retired At 26!*, she suggests that "We have
been socially manipulated into thinking that labor and leisure
are separate events that happen at different stages of our lives.
And so we have chopped life into three pieces. The first part of
life is set aside for school. Once that is finished, the second part
begins. We go to work.........Meanwhile, we try to squeeze
happiness in on the weekends. Then there is the third piece of
our lives. The grand finale we've all been waiting to have for
sixty-five years. Retirement. They have hyped us up about
crossing this imaginary finish line ever since our very first day
of work........I didn't want to spend forty years trying to earn
the privilege of becoming free one day. I wanted to be free
*to*day. So, I revolutionized the meaning of retirement in my
life. I decided it meant something different, something prom-
ising, something hopeful, and something to partake of right
now! *I integrated enjoyment and work into the overall meaning of
my life!*"

Ms. Tyson chose to make her cherished dreams come true sooner, rather than later. Whatever your dreams, make sure that you hold on to them and do everything in your power to make them happen now, rather than at some undefined point in the future. Every job, every pursuit has some negatives. Choose to focus on the positive. Focus on what's good about what you do in life. Wherever you are—be there, making sure that your attention is firmly fixed on the present moment.

Establish a Blueprint

Every goal goes through an evolutionary process that involves three main stages:

- First of all, your goals begin life as embryonic concepts in your imagination.

- Secondly, they take shape, as you begin to organize your dreams into plans.

- Thirdly, your plans become reality, as your actions describe their outcome.

It's time to get down to the details and give some substance to your dreams. So, grab your pen and paper or, better still, get yourself some goal-setting software; it's much more comprehensive and considerably more flexible than traditional methods, because it allows you to update and modify your goals quickly and easily, in the light of experience. Remember, goals become far more tangible and are more likely to be achieved if you can see them, either on a piece of paper or a computer screen.

Acknowledged goals expert Brian Tracy writes down his major goals every day, focusing clearly on what he must achieve in order to make progress. When we have our goals in front of us all the time, we will start to believe in them, to live them, and to create their reality. Our goals will begin to manifest themselves, because we'll see them when we believe them.

Remember, to be successful, our goals must be written down, personal, realistic, achievable, challenging, rewarding, measurable, clear, specific and vivid. In addition, our goals must be time limited, otherwise they would remain dreams, as we won't hold ourselves accountable to their realization. Most importantly, our goals must be accompanied by a burning desire and a commitment. Phrase your goals in positive terms. Focus on what you will do to achieve your goals, rather than what you will give up doing. Your subconscious mind will accept whatever instructions you give it; good or bad. The more positive the directions, the more likely you will be to arrive at your destination. Learn to distinguish the urgent from the important. Urgency makes us predominantly reactive, and that's not a good thing. Some issues will fight for your attention and you'll be tempted to deal with them immediately just to be rid of them. Ask yourself whether these interruptions are important. Will they help you achieve your goals, or are they simply urgent, attention-seeking tasks? Is their pursuit vital to your future success? Do they address the underlying needs that you must tackle in order to feed your long-term growth?

By shifting your focus to deal with what is important, you will find yourself becoming increasingly proactive in your outlook and your day-to-day activities will begin to align with your higher goals. Don't allow people and events to distract you from your purpose. If the route to goal becomes too cluttered, you won't be able to see what you're aiming for. Concentrate on defining all that you do in relation to your goals and a path will clear itself automatically. If it doesn't fit the goal, don't do it.

> *L* *ife will not go according to plan, if you do not have a plan*
>
> **GARY RYAN BLAIR—THE GOALS GUY**

Don't be tempted to assume responsibility for goals that fall outside of your sphere of influence. Think small, work on changing what's close to you, concentrate your efforts where you will see the effect of your actions. Gradually your achievements will build until you find yourself in a position to manipulate the bigger picture. You may not be able to change the direction of your nation's defence policy, but you could have a positive influence on a problem that exists close to home.

Make sure that your goals are detailed. Instead of writing down that you would like to own a vacation property, describe its location, its size, its style, the view from the front of the house, the nearby lake, river, mountains, forest or sea. How much money are you going to need to purchase and renovate it? The clearer the picture that you paint for your subconscious mind, the closer you become to achieving your goal.[11]

Goals must also be well communicated. Many of us are not just setting goals for ourselves. You may be responsible for developing a set of goals that will influence an entire organization. Communicate your goals clearly and you'll empower a group of people with understanding, a sense of worth and a shared purpose.[12] And remember, few worthwhile goals are achieved alone; don't be afraid to ask for some assistance along the way. Make sure that the goals you choose are always close to your heart. A goal that sounds good, but doesn't coincide with what you really want out of life, will be without substance and is likely to fail at the first hint of opposition. If you haven't convinced yourself about the value and importance of your goals, you have little hope of convincing anyone to adopt them and call them their own. Goals that form a strong connection with the person you really are, and the principles that you value most, will be driven by an unequalled strength of purpose. And, just before you go to sleep at night, remind yourself of your most important goals. You may be sleeping, but your mind's still working. When you wake up, your goals will be your top priority.

Prepare Your Plan

Now that you've made the choice to get started on a plan that will help you define and achieve your goals, why not consider some of the following suggestions to help give shape to your outline? This is by no means an exhaustive list, but it should spark some new ideas.

Analyze your Situation

Take stock of your current situation

Identify your Desires

What have you always dreamed of doing?

Recognize your Reasons

Ask yourself why you want to achieve your goals

Record your Goals

Are they specific, clear and vivid? Do they have the characteristics of worthwhile goals?

List your Obstacles

Identify the challenges you may face before you reach your goals

Fill in your Gaps

Pinpoint the knowledge you need to acquire in order to succeed

Identify your Collaborators

Find the people that can assist you in accomplishing your goals

Prepare your Battle plan

List all the activities required to achieve your goals

Set your Deadlines

Establish time limits to reflect short, mid and long-term goals.

Set mini deadlines and reward yourself for achievement

Visualize and Emotionalize

Create a clear mental picture of the goal and imagine how you will feel about the result

Reveal your Determination

Remember that whatever you set out to do will require persistent effort to be successful

Take Time to Review

When you've finished the first outline of your goals, I'd encourage you to set it aside for a while. Come back to it later with fresh eyes, to weed out the imperfections and review the priorities you've set for yourself. Ask yourself whether your goals are realistic but, at the same time, ensure that you have also set your sights high enough and that you're thinking big enough. If a goal is going to be worthwhile it's also going to be a bit of a stretch. Don't lose sight of your strategic objectives. It would be so easy to get distracted by the tactical moves that you have included in your battle plan and loosen your grip on the loud and proud goals that are going to revolutionize your life. It may be more comforting to become absorbed by the minute details of a plan, but unless you keep your eyes on the road ahead, you're likely to take a wrong turn.

As you scan your list of goals, both large and small, make sure that none of them are contradictory. If you've set yourself the goal of reducing pollution levels from the traffic in your city, it would be inadvisable to aim to become an SUV owner. When you're establishing goals that require financing, make sure that they are in line with your current and projected income levels; don't take a tour of the mansion, when you should really be saving for a condo. Your goals should reflect your circumstances and core values as closely as possible. The more integrated your goals and your values, the more likely you are to achieve them and uphold them.

Do your goals adequately reflect the multiple personalities involved in your life? Do you think that you have drawn up a balanced set of goals? Have you set goals that reflect your sense of purpose at work, as well as your objectives as a member of a family? Have you drawn up a checklist of issues that you must address concerning your health, your lifestyle and your habits? Do you feel that you understand the kind of friend you aim to be and the type of friendships you will cultivate? And are you paying enough attention to what goes on inside your head? What are you doing to feed your spirit and your need for life-long learning?

It is vitally important that you set aside time to review your goals frequently. Do this daily, if you can. Never take your eye off the ball; by keeping firmly focused on the objectives of the game, your activities will be far more likely to show up on the scoreboard. Try and make a habit of relating your everyday life to the goals you have set for yourself. Throughout your day, each time you make a decision, ask yourself whether that decision takes you closer to, or further away from your goals. Goal setting is not an isolated exercise; its aim is not to download the data, archive it and then simply forget about it, or hope that somehow it will magically take care of itself. Circumstances are bound to change, and you and your goals must be flexible enough to reflect these changes. If you need to modify any of your goals, just go ahead and do it (this is where the software comes in handy). But don't forget that you'll also have to update your action plan and possibly even redefine some of your interim deadlines. By constantly adjusting your course, you will make swifter progress and be more likely to reach your destination on time.[13]

Vision: Run That By Me Again

- **Document your development**
  Where have you been, what have you done & where are you going?

- **Make a personal checklist**
  How do you live, love & learn? What legacy will you leave?

- **Turn self-acceptance into self-awareness**
  The mistakes of your past don't have to define your future

- **Restore balance**
  Examine career, health, family life, friendships, mind and soul

- **Map out your goals**
  Write down what you want to achieve & find a way to visualize it

- **Think about 'retiring' now**
  Create the state of mind that combines work with enjoyment

- **Concentrate on what you *can* do**
  Accent the positive & focus on your sphere of influence

- **Communicate your objectives**
  If you're sharing your goals, take plenty of time to deliver the message

- **Develop goals to reflect your values**
  If you're connected to your goals, they'll be driven by strength of purpose

- **Define your deadlines**
  Sticking to time limits turns dreams into reality

- **Prepare a Plan**
  The actions you'll take, the obstacles you'll face, & the help you'll need

- **Review, review, review**
  Make time to review, challenge & improve the goals you've set for yourself

3

Have Confidence In Yourself

"If you can walk you can dance.
If you can talk you can sing."
ZIMBABWEAN PROVERB

The Fear Factor

Perhaps the biggest barrier to personal or collective success is fear. We're afraid of our own potential, frightened of succeeding at the expense of others, terrified of what other people might think if we fail. Our level of commitment is handicapped by approach-avoidance and self-sabotage. Like the hesitant child on the edge of a pool, we know we're going to love it when we're in the water but we can't bring ourselves to jump in. Many of us are too scared to step outside the comforting boundaries of a familiar culture, an inherited education and a collection of unquestioned experiences. We become anxious when we're asked to look beyond recognizable horizons to explore new possibilities. We're afraid to rise up to meet a challenge, in case the responsibilities prove to be too much to handle. There are those amongst us who would choose lifelong anonymity over the slightest hint of a chance of success, fearing the consequences of failure and the agony of disappointment. But we're not alone. Anyone who has ever been successful has experienced the same kind of terror.

*A*nything I've ever done that ultimately was
worthwhile initially scared me to death

BETTY BENDER—COMMUNICATION CONSULTANT

If we were to be honest about our fears, we'd probably have to admit that the biggest obstacle we all face is our fear of people, and what they think about us. Consider this: what other people think of you and your dreams is none of your business. It's their business. There will always be people waiting to squash your dreams, wrapped up in their own insecurities, envious of your potential. If they can't see it in themselves, they won't see it in you either, and they will hope you fail because your failure would validate their own inactivity. Non-affirming relationships can be extremely harmful. Concentrate instead on surrounding yourself with support. There will always be someone eager to burst your bubble but, as Eleanor Roosevelt said, "No one can make you feel inferior without your consent." If it's absolutely necessary to kill a dream, do it yourself. Don't let somebody else manipulate your future.

Keep away from people who try to belittle your ambitions. Small people always do that, but the really great ones make you feel that you too can become great

MARK TWAIN—WRITER

Potential Failure

We're so afraid of the consequences of failure that we're tempted to abandon hope, accept our imperfections, learn to live with them, and even develop their potential as excuses to do nothing. As Les Brown suggests in his powerful seminar *The Power to Change*, "When we argue for our limitations we get to keep them." While our failings and limitations might define our humanity, they don't give us permission to stagnate. We're all less than perfect, but that's okay. Again, perfection doesn't exist but progress wants to happen. What we're aiming for is growth. We're attempting to transform, not conform. In the previous chapter, we established that it is important to recognize weaknesses as well as strengths and to come to terms with the kind of imperfections that we can't change. But don't confuse self-acceptance with permission. Don't validate complacency through resignation. Instead, turn self-acceptance into self-awareness and use it as a springboard to your new future. The saying may be well worn, but it still holds true, "If you always do what you've always done, you'll always get what you've always got."

Consult not your fears but your hopes and your dreams. Think not about your frustrations, but about your unfulfilled potential. Concern yourself not with what you tried and failed in, but with what is still possible for you to do

POPE JOHN XXIII—28.X.1958—3.VI.1963

Once you understand that failure is simply a small detour on the journey to success, the less concerned you'll be about failing. If you haven't failed in the past and you're not failing now, chances are that you're not succeeding either. Encourage yourself to overcome your fear of failure, tell yourself that you're fully prepared to fail as many times as it takes to succeed, and you'll find that you stop worrying about what people think. Force yourself to take some risks. The greatest love and the greatest achievements involve the greatest risk. Bobby Kennedy once said that, "Only those who dare to fail greatly can ever achieve greatly." Surround yourself with the kind of people who will blame you for not trying, rather than blame you for failing. Expose your ideas to a small number of people you can trust, because, when you're dealing with the fear of failure, it's important to ask for help. It can be overwhelming to face fear alone. When you do lose, just make sure that you don't lose the lesson. Force yourself to confront previous failures. You'll better understand why they happened and you'll be better equipped to leave them behind. The greater your understanding, the more adept you'll become at avoiding the mistakes of the past. Everybody falls down. And most people do it publicly. What matters is how fast you get back up.

> *Success is the ability to go from one failure to another with no loss of enthusiasm*
>
> SIR WINSTON CHURCHILL—STATESMAN, POLITICIAN & LEADER

Lincoln Could Have Been a Loser

Abraham Lincoln, 16th President of the United States of America, is remembered by the world for the vital leadership role he played in preserving the Union during the American Civil War. He is also credited with pioneering the process that led to the end of slavery in the US. A man from humble origins, he created an enduring and highly visible legacy and, for many, epitomizes the definition of success. As jobs go, ruling a country gripped by civil war, or raising your head above the parapet to advocate emancipation could hardly be considered a walk in the park. But these feats were nothing in comparison to the spectacular failures, multiple setbacks and numerous hardships that Lincoln overcame throughout his life.

Before he reached his twenties, Abraham Lincoln had already lost his younger brother, Thomas, who died in infancy, his mother Nancy, who died from milk sickness when he was only 9 years old and his elder sister, Sarah, who died in childbirth. As if that wasn't enough, death also claimed his sweetheart, Sarah Rutledge in 1835. Unfortunately, this macabre theme was to continue into his married life, with only one of his four children surviving into adulthood.

Sheer persistence and determination led this man with only 12 months of formal schooling to the White House in 1860, to assume the nation's highest office. Take a look at the list of failures that helped get him there:[14]

THE YEAR   THE CHALLENGE

1832   Young Abraham, who'd failed to follow in his father's footsteps on the family farm, distinguished himself this year by losing his job and making an unsuccessful run for the Illinois State Legislature

1833   Abe's business venture (he ran a store) went bottom up

1836   Lincoln momentarily failed to hold on to his sanity and had a nervous breakdown. This probably had a lot to do with losing his girlfriend the year before

1838   By this time, our man has made it to the State Legislature only to be defeated in his quest to become Speaker

1843   Lincoln makes his first bid for Congress, but fails to secure the nomination

1848   Congressman Lincoln (he made it to the House of Representatives in 1846) fails to seek re-nomination

1849   He seeks appointment to the United States Land Office but meets with rejection

1854   Abraham sets his sights on the Senate but (you guessed it) his bid is unsuccessful

1856   Friends support him in his bid for the Republican Vice Presidential nomination but Lincoln fails to be chosen

1858   Once again the Senate eludes him

1860   Makes it to The White House!

Permission to Succeed

Before we can persuade anyone else of the power we have to transform our lives, we've got to convince ourselves that it's possible, and that we deserve it. Lincoln refused to see himself as a failure, and his self-confidence eventually rewarded him handsomely. According to a traditional Hasidic saying, "The man who has confidence in himself gains the confidence of others." We have to give ourselves permission to succeed. If you accept the fact that we're all here for a purpose, then it follows that we're each perfectly suited for our destiny. We have to overcome the fear of what might happen if we follow our destined path. We must stop worrying about future possibilities. There'll be plenty of time to deal with success when it happens. What's important now is to grab hold of the challenge and run with it, before someone else does.

> *B**elieve in yourself! Have faith in your abilities!*
> *Without a humble but reasonable confidence in*
> *your own powers you cannot be successful or happy*
>
> **NORMAN VINCENT PEALE**
>
> **—CLERGYMAN, AUTHOR & APOSTLE OF SELF-ESTEEM**

No one deserves success more than you do, but people will try to persuade you otherwise. Some believe that the pursuit of personal success is a tainted goal. These are the people who are uncomfortable with the idea of wealth and prosperity, whatever form it takes. They'll tell you that your success will be a hollow victory, won at the expense of someone else's happiness.

It can be a persuasive argument if you've always lived in a society that is defined by contrasts, if you've been raised by a culture that thinks in terms of scarcity rather than abundance. But that kind of thinking has grown very stale. As long as the achievement of personal goals doesn't harm anyone else, there is plenty of room for us all to become successful. But why stop there? If we can also make it our mission to help others as a bi-product of our own success, those negative tongues will be forever silenced. If your vision of success supports a responsible and heartfelt set of beliefs and values, it doesn't matter whether its aim is financial or spiritual, focused on family, friends, or career. And, it doesn't matter how many people are chasing the dream. Success isn't a pizza that disappears once you've divided up the portions. If our global society has taught us anything, it's that we're redefining boundaries faster than ever before. The pizza is getting bigger and we're all entitled to a slice!

> *It is never too late to be what you might have been*
> GEORGE ELIOT—A WOMAN IN ADVANCE OF HER TIME

Patterns of Behaviour

But it's not only a fear of people that's holding us back, is it? The way we've learned to view the world has a lot to do with our perception of what is, or isn't possible, what we fear and what we embrace. This worldview is often referred to as a paradigm. Futuristic thinker, Joel Barker, was responsible for bringing the concept of paradigms to the business world when he began popularizing the theory of paradigm shifts and vision back in 1975. The word paradigm isn't a very descriptive one, but it refers to a person's unique perspective on life. It's the emotional DNA that results from your upbringing, education, your life experiences and the choices you've made to date. Think of a paradigm as a camera viewfinder. You chose to frame the picture, but it doesn't necessarily reflect the reality of the scene. The picture could look very different with someone else behind the lens. If you want to transform your life, you're going to have to shift some of those paradigms and create a whole new photo album.

Leading behavioural researchers once suggested that as many as 3 out of every 4 thoughts we think are negative and counter-productive. During the first eighteen years of our lives, if we grew up in fairly average, reasonably positive homes, we were told "No!" at least 150,000 times.[15] Blanchard Training & Development, one of the group of Ken Blanchard Companies, suggests that we need to hear 12 positive comments to overcome a single negative. In their book, *The 7 Principles for Making Marriage Work*, co-authors Dr. J.M. Gottman and Nan Silver tell us that the common denominator in successful marriages is a relationship in which positive gestures and statements outweigh criticisms by 5:1.[16] Whatever the statistics, it's clear that negative communication can have a very destructive effect.

All of us can remember comments from our childhood, throwaway lines made casually by teachers, parents, siblings, relatives, classmates, community leaders that have profoundly affected our self-perception throughout our adult lives. As a result of someone else's definition of our own skills, we can grow up believing that we'll never be artistic or scientific or athletic or beautiful etc. etc. As a result of our own definition of someone else's skills, they can grow up believing that they'll never make the grade either. You know the story, and it works both ways. But we can't let what other people think define who we are, because they have every chance of being wrong.

The way we all conduct our lives is an expression of what we believe, based on our personal history of values, influences and experiences. Throughout time, we have also defined ourselves collectively through our shared perception of the reality we live through. Each age; Mediaeval, Renaissance, Industrial, Information, has been both driven and limited by a communal sense of what is either possible, or unattainable. In his book, *The Four Agreements*, Don Miguel Ruiz suggests that "we are born with the capacity to learn how to dream, and the humans who live before us teach us how to dream the way society dreams...how to behave in society: what to believe and what not to believe; what is acceptable and what is not acceptable; what is good and what is bad; what is beautiful and what is ugly; what is right and what is wrong."

Too often we base our vision of the future on our self-limiting memories of the past. If we haven't seen it work before, or we've been told it can't be done, we can't imagine it working now, or at any point in the future. But, if you're committed to the vision, there's no room for the failure. Before April 1954 no man had been physically capable of running a mile in less than four minutes. Globally, all in the field of the study of human potential believed that it couldn't be done. Then Roger

Bannister broke that barrier and proved to the world it *could* be done. Since that moment, thousands have achieved the same or better. Once people see that something is possible, they believe they can do it too.[17] The trick is to be ahead of the curve. Enrich your dream using your imagination instead of your memory. Instead of running a mile in someone else's shoes, be like Roger Bannister. Convince yourself that it's possible and set the pace yourself. Similarly, in the early 1970s, inventor Danny Hillis was speaking to a large audience at the Hilton Hotel in New York City. He predicted that one day, there would be more microprocessors than people in the United States. Everyone laughed and one audience member asked, "What are you going to do with all those microprocessors? It's not as if you need one in every doorknob!" Today, every Hilton hotel room has a microporcessor in its doorknob.[18] What belonged to the realms of science fiction three decades or so ago, is now unquestioned fact. Anything is possible. As motivational author, Wayne Dyer said, "You'll see it when you believe it."

> **W**hat is now proved was once only imagined
>
> **WILLIAM BLAKE—POET, ARTIST, ENGRAVER & PUBLISHER**

Information Leads to Transformation

If we are going to acquire the kind of confidence that will point us in the direction of a successful life, we must be willing to embrace the learning curve. Wherever you currently find yourself on that curve, there's always another bend in the road ahead of you. You're going to need to learn to stick to the road. But, don't expect to be cornering like a pro from the outset. All achievement has its origins in the mind, but be prepared to lose what you don't use. If you don't exercise your mind, it'll become lazy and inactive. Stephen Covey refers to the learning process as "sharpening the saw", Abraham Lincoln "sharpening the axe". However you look at it, the quicker the mind, the faster you'll achieve success. Recognize the importance of continuous learning, to develop your skills, your self-awareness and your understanding of others. It has always impressed me that the world's greatest golfer continues to take lessons! In the eyes of most mortal golfers, Tiger Woods has perfected his talents beyond the realms of reasonable imagination. You could argue that there's no one and nothing left to teach him. Woods, however, has understood that the degree of progress he makes with his game depends on his ability to acquire new skills and to practise them. When you are more knowledgeable or more skilled, you become more confident. When you are more confident, you become more competent. It was Bob Proctor who first brought to my attention a definition of skills progression, known as the Four Levels of Competence. You can apply this model to any learning situation you will ever encounter:

The Four Levels of Competence

Unconscious Incompetence: This is the domain of the blissfully ignorant. We simply don't know that we don't know. We're adrift in the cosmic void. We're totally unaware of the knowledge, the skill, the territory, the culture, or the opinion.

We may be misinterpreting much of what goes on around us.

Conscious Incompetence: We begin to panic. But it's a healthy level of fear. We now know that we don't know, and we're feeling exposed. We realize that our information and understanding is lacking, and that we do not have the skill to leverage what little we have. We're barely hanging on but we start to think about making choices.

Conscious Competence: We're in the zone. We know that we know. We know where we are and how to get to where we want to be. We're in the game, in the moment. We're gathering the knowledge we need to fill the voids, plus we've gained the confidence to alter our previous patterns of behaviour and thinking. It doesn't come naturally yet, but we're putting newfound skills into practice and learning to integrate them into everything we do.

Unconscious Competence: Now it's second nature. We are known for what we know. We have become experts and can apply our knowledge and skills to a situation intuitively and effortlessly. Our actions are dictated by our past experience. Edgar Degas once said, "Only when he no longer knows what he is doing does the painter do good things."

Degas wasn't alone in his sentiments. It is generally considered that we should all be aiming for Level 4, the state of Unconscious Competence, where our skills are instinctive and our responses are effortless. I disagree. There is a fine line between Unconscious Competence and the slippery slide back to Unconscious Incompetence. If you're not careful, before you know where you are, once again you'll be adrift in the cosmic void. Why? Because you'll have started taking things for granted and you will lose focus. Competence is like humility; the day you think you have it is the day you need it. Too often people 'perfect' their skills and forget that learning is a lifelong responsibility. They become complacent and lose their edge. Take your lead from Tiger Woods. When he is competing in a tournament, this golfer enjoys moments of Unconscious Competence, playing instinctively. Between these moments and between tournaments, he knows that he must return to the realms of Conscious Competence. In order to stay in the zone and maintain his edge he has to keep sharpening the saw. Don't underestimate the importance of Level 3, the state of Conscious Competence. It is here that you'll be confident of your own abilities, hungry for more, and still humble enough to stay focused.

> *As long as you're green you're growing. As soon as you're ripe, you start to rot*
>
> RAY KROC—FOUNDER OF MACDONALDS

Just Do It

If we don't compete, we can't win. Most of us have already worked out what we *should* be doing, but we're all waiting until we're less busy, more focused, better equipped to pursue our dreams. We need to admit to ourselves that there'll never be a right time to do anything and, unless we marry thought with action, our most cherished aspirations will remain unfulfilled. For most of us, it's not a question of ability but rather one of determination—not *can* we, but *will* we get up and get in the game? There will always be obstacles that stand between you and your happiness. You will never be fully prepared to launch your new venture. And there will forever be people watching from the sidelines, waiting for you to plant your face in the mud. Circumstances will never be ideal. But, as Les Brown says, "You've got to do what you can, where you are, with what you have".[19]

> *The meek will inherit the earth, in nice 6 x 3 plots*
> ROBERT HEINLEIN—SCI FI GRANDMASTER

Too many of us suffer from the paralysis of analysis. Because we're so carefully dissecting our options, so busily examining the problems and the pitfalls, overthinking every last detail, we lose sight of our opportunities, or convince ourselves that we can't ever overcome the obstacles. When my daughter tells me tearfully, "Daddy, I can't do it!" I make it my mission to convince her that she can, that she's "The Little Engine That Could", because I have every confidence in her abilities to overcome her fears and her frustrations. Why can't we be so confident about our own abilities? As adults, it's very comforting to immerse ourselves in the logistics of planning, preparation and evaluation. Analytical tasks such as these put off the inevitable moment when we will have to make a decision, take some action and tell ourselves that we *can* do it. Procrastination is the thief of time, the thief of life, and it could well steal your opportunity for success. Of course, we know that every outstanding performance we've ever seen has been well rehearsed, but there comes a time when the practising stops and the performers walk boldly onto the stage.

> *What convinces is conviction. Believe in the argument you are advancing. If you don't you're as good as dead. The other person will sense something isn't there and no chain of reasoning, no matter how logical, or elegant, or brilliant will win your case for you*
>
> LYNDON BAINES JOHNSON
> —36TH PRESIDENT OF THE UNITED STATES

Commit! Tremendous power is unleashed the moment a decision is made. Every new beginning starts with a single step, and once you take yours, you'll be surprised how quickly your plan will come to fruition. Avoid being branded a *lifer*, the kind of person who is sentenced to stagnate, living each day much as the one before. If you want to come home with the trophies, you've got to play the sport. When you're doing, you're winning. God didn't put us on this earth to watch TV; God put us here to be on TV! We've got to be prepared to start taking some risks. If we take risks, we *might* fail but if we take no risks, we're sure to fail. You can't marry the princess without killing the dragon. If we take a few steps outside of the comfort zone, take a few more chances, we've got more chances of winning.[20]

*T*he best way to predict the future is to create it

PETER DRUCKER

—SOCIAL COMMENTATOR & BUSINESS PHILOSOPHER

A friend once said to me that wherever thought goes, energy flows. And often, when I have been wrestling with the pros and cons of an embryonic idea, if I shift my attention from analysis to action, I find that I have a much clearer understanding of what I must do to reach my goal. I think it was the motivational trainer, James Rae who said, "When the intent is clear, the method will appear." The decision to do something can be surprisingly liberating, however fearful you may be about the outcome. Things may get a bit messy as you head for your goal but you'll be astonished how many people will be there to help you once you've become decisive. "Don't wait for the light to appear at the end of the tunnel, run down there and light the damn thing yourself."[21] In doing so, you'll probably find that you've lit the way for a number of other people, who'll be eternally grateful for your determination to make it happen.

So, set aside the research, the endless discussions, the everlasting meetings and go with your gut reaction. "If we listened to our intellect, we'd never have a love affair. We'd never have a friendship. We'd never go into business, because we'd be cynical. Well, that's nonsense. You've got to jump off cliffs all the time and build your wings on the way down."[22]

*E*ither you think you can or you think you can't. Either way you're right

HENRY FORD—MOTORIST & INDUSTRIALIST

Are You Fit For the Challenge?

The better you feel, the more confident you will be. It's no secret that a healthy body produces a sharp mind, but only about 20% of us exercise regularly. We are what we eat, and with a tendency to supersize everything, over 60% of North Americans weigh too much. Approximately 280,000 adult deaths in the United States each year are attributable to obesity.[23] Some of us avoid exercise in adult life because we consider ourselves to have been school sports failures. We associate sports with humiliation rather than pleasure, so we consider exercise to be a punishment. Without a gym teacher breathing down our necks, many of us succumb to the lure of the couch. We find excuses. In fact, we actually choose *not* to be fit. There are others amongst us who consider ourselves far too busy to fit exercise into our daily schedules, so we go on crash diets instead.

It is not the purpose of this book to design a program for the 80% of you who are not exercising, but it is important to underline the benefits of optimum health. You only get one body. What are you going to do with yours? Some people choose to treat their bodies like temples, others like amusement parks. You don't need to go to either extreme, but if you take even a moderately active responsibility for your health, you will have a profound effect on your quality of life and on the amounts of effort, energy and enthusiasm you can apply to living it. You don't need to be an athlete to be fit and healthy, anyone can do it.

Fitter people are happier, more confident people, and a well-maintained body lives longer. If you eat nutritious food, rather than junk, and if you exercise regularly and realistically, both your body and your mind will perform better. Exercise increases oxygen flow to the brain, boosting optimism, effective stress management, clarity of thought and the ability to learn. A well-exercised body has a stronger immune system and sleeps more restfully. As a result someone who exercises regularly is more relaxed and better able to balance the demands of each day. Unless you take full responsibility for your health and fitness, you will never be able to assume full responsibility for your potential.

According to David Patchell-Evans, five time Canadian rowing champion and president and CEO of GoodLife Fitness Clubs, Canada's largest and fastest-growing fitness empire, exercise can be held responsible for all of the following:[24]

- Improving circulation and lowering blood pressure
- Improving your posture
- Decreasing the chances of developing osteoporosis
- Lowering your risk of death from cancer
- Improving your resistance to infectious diseases
- Increasing the efficiency of your sweat glands
- Enabling you to stay warmer in colder environments
- Alleviating constipation
- Enhancing sexual performance
- Helping you move from left- to right-brain thinking
- Making people look at you and say, "Wow! You look great!"

With all of the above in mind:
- **Make an honest list of everything you have eaten today**
- **Calculate the time you have spent exercising this week**
- **Estimate the number of hours sleep you got last night**
- **Check out when you last went for a physical check up**
- **Set yourself some lifestyle, health and fitness goals**

Borrow an Idea

The world's richest man, who became a billionaire at the age of 31, has achieved enormous wealth by following where others have shown the way. Yale Professor of Computer Science, David Gelernter, has described Bill Gates, co-founder and chief helmsman at Microsoft as "...no visionary; he is a technology groupie with a genius for showing up, for being in the right place at the right time." Microsoft's first product launch in the 1970s combined BASIC, an existing programming language, with the Altair, a prototype PC. Both were someone else's idea. Gates provided the inspiration and business savvy to bring them together and create an extremely powerful late 20th Century phenomenon. When IBM hired Microsoft to develop a PC operating system in the 1980s, Gates bought Q-DOS from a Seattle (that city again) computer company and reworked it for the PC. MS-DOS quickly became the operating standard. Once more, all Gates had done was to act as broker between ideas. By the following decade, Microsoft had managed to perfect its own version of the user-friendly software developed by Apple for its Macintosh computers and Bill Gates took the PC world by storm with Microsoft Windows. When the

Internet took hold, Gates held back. He waited for Netscape to perfect web browsing technology and watched as Sun Microsystems developed Java, the Internet programming language. With the benefit of the experience accumulated by his competitors, Gates licensed the first copy of Internet Explorer from a company by the name of Spyglass. Today, Microsoft is the world's most dominant supplier of Web browsers.[25]

Similarly, Sam Walton's business took off when he engineered a marriage between a cash register and a database. Neither partner brought anything new to the marriage but together they had an astounding effect on Wal-Mart's business success. By connecting cash registers to databases he was able to track stock with minimum human intervention and in doing so, changed the face of retailing. His reward? An annual global turnover that resembles the GDP of Austria.[26]

*E**ighty percent of success is showing up***
WOODY ALLEN—ACTOR, COMEDIAN & DIRECTOR

If the experience of Bill Gates and Sam Walton is anything to go by, you don't need to spend the rest of your life searching for the perfect original idea. Adapting somebody else's, or brokering existing skills and technologies seems to work just as well. The key to success may not rest so much on the idea itself, as in the courage to execute it and the ability to pop up to claim ownership of it at just the right moment. Often it's enough to find yourself an old idea and to add value to it.

Motivator and author, Bob Proctor introduced me to the recorded inspirations of Doug Wead, former advisor to the presidential administrations of Ronald Reagan and George H. Bush. I'd like to share with you some of his observations about Columbus' voyages of discovery because, as Wead points out, the man was immortalized for changing the world when, in reality, he was really sailing into waters that had already been charted. Christopher Columbus is credited with the discovery of the New World, (an accomplishment that he pulled off using a ship the size of a tennis court). As a result of his trip to the Americas, he discovered tobacco (although he didn't realize it at the time) and brought back countless new foods to Europe, including chilies, corn, potatoes, pumpkin, peanuts, chocolate, vanilla, blueberries, sunflowers and spices. (It is also sobering to think that the pre-Columbian population of central America, which amounted to 30 million people, was reduced to a mere 3 million when Columbus and his crew imported diseases like yellow fever, cholera and mumps.) It's important to remember that he didn't truly discover the New World, which was, after all, already home to 30 million people. For a start, it had already been spotted by a number of missionary expeditions. Lief Erikson had also visited Newfoundland in 1000 AD, and a group of French fishermen had beaten Columbus to the continent about 200 years before he eventually sailed the ocean blue. You couldn't even say that Columbus was the sharpest tool in the shed. He wasn't a good sailor or navigator and his nautical experience was limited, with only one previous voyage under his belt (and that wasn't even as captain). He didn't possess the wealth to fund the expedition and he didn't have the necessary scientific knowledge to interpret the novelties of the new territories. What he did have was a dream, plus the ability, the confidence and the commitment to gather the experts he needed to achieve it. What he did have was the persistence to chase King Ferdinand and Queen Isabella for the funding. What he did have was the courage to quit discussing the pros and cons of departure and just set sail. And he was obstinate enough to ignore advice to turn back when provisions were running dangerously low. Columbus was the catalyst that provided the value-add. The rest, as they say, is history.

> *There are three kinds of people: those who make things happen, those who watch things happen, and those who ask, 'what happened?'*
>
> CASEY STENGEL—BASEBALL HALL-OF-FAMER

If You Think You Can't

If you're tempted to doubt your own capabilities, why not draw your inspiration from some high-profile success stories, of people who achieved greatness in spite of everything?

Charles M. Schulz

The only modern American comic strip artist to be given a retrospective at the Louvre had his drawings rejected by his high school yearbook committee. Schulz also failed several times before he finally sold 'Peanuts' to the United Feature Syndicate.[27]

Babe Ruth

This immortal baseball player spent his childhood years in an orphanage and then struck out 1,330 times on his way to 714 home runs and baseball immortality.

Elvis Presley

The King himself was fired from the Grand Ole Opry after only one performance and told by the manager, "You ain't goin' nowhere, son. Better get y'all job back drivin' a truck."

Oprah Winfrey

The Queen of chat remained undeterred when she was fired from her job as a TV reporter. With the words "You're not fit for TV," still ringing in her ears, she went on to become one of the most popular and successful women in television.

Sir Edmund Hillary

This man conquered Mount Everest after three failed attempts. People said, "You've conquered the mountain," and Hillary said, "No, I've conquered myself."[28]

> *The people who make it in this life look around for the circumstances they want and if they can't find them, they create them*
>
> **GEORGE BERNARD SHAW—ANGLO-IRISH PLAYWRIGHT**

Confidence: Run That By Me Again

- **Conquer your fear of new territory**
  Don't be afraid of your own potential

- **Don't be afraid of people**
  What other people think of you and your dreams is not your concern, it's theirs

- **Become familiar with failure**
  The closer you come to failure, the quicker you'll meet success

- **Give yourself permission to succeed**
  Nobody deserves success more than you do

- **Create a plentiful environment**
  Avoid thoughts of scarcity and think confidently in terms of abundance

- **Change your point of view**
  Be prepared to alter your emotional programming

- **Don't rely on your memory**
  Avoid self-limiting memories & embrace infinite possibilities

- **Learn to take care of yourself**
  Follow the learning curve and use information to unleash transformation

- **Be conscious of your competence**
  Know where you are & how to get to where you want to be

- **Just do it**
  Avoid the paralysis of analysis

- **Shape up**
  Fit, healthy people are more confident and productive

- **Adopt an idea**
  Just because it's been done before doesn't mean you can't do it again

4

Recognize Your Responsibility

---

*"Few will have the greatness to bend
history itself, but each of us can work to
change a small portion of events, and in
the total of all those acts will be written
the history of this generation."*

JOHN F. KENNEDY, 35TH PRESIDENT OF THE UNITED STATES

Feel the Difference

If you've been given a life, you might as well use it! Nobody else has the ability to fulfill your destiny. We've each been given something to add to this world that wasn't here before we arrived and it's time to answer the call. We weren't put on this planet just to keep things the way they are. As Steve Jobs says, "Let's make a dent in the Universe." We're supposed to be making a difference, leaving a legacy, contributing to our communities. Isn't it our responsibility to be productive, to make progress and to add worth? Don't we want to leave the world looking greater, better and more beautiful than we found it? So, what are we waiting for? Why all the hesitation to get started?

Most of you reading this book have the luxury of living in a culture that considers political, economic and intellectual freedom to be a birthright, not a privilege. As long as we harm no one in the process, we are entirely at liberty to pursue our hopes, our dreams, our projects and our schemes. If we suffer from anything, it's affluenza! We're caught in an epidemic of over consumption (and it could be the disease that kills us all). In contrast, more than 1.5 billion people worldwide lack decent, affordable housing. That's almost one quarter of the world's population. If you lived in Zambia, your life expectancy at birth would be all of 35 years, your chances of dying in infancy, around 10%. In the UK or the US, you could expect to live more than double that length of time to around the age of 77; in Canada you'd be more likely to reach 80. And infant mortality rates in these affluent countries barely register, at around 5 for every 1,000 births.[29] The reality is that much of the rest of the world continues to suffer the deprivation of either political repression, or economic disadvantage.

We will have to repent in this generation not merely for the vitriolic words and actions of the bad people, but for the appalling silence of the good people

MARTIN LUTHER KING JR.—STATESMAN

I fail to understand why we, with all our privileges, are the ones hesitating to do something of significance with our lives. In many countries throughout the world, people are struggling to satisfy the most basic of needs. They are desperately trying to feed themselves and their families. They are striving to provide shelter and gain access to a basic education. At the same time they fear for their safety and the security of their loved ones in the face of oppression and war. They are failing to secure even the most fundamental of health needs. Is it not, therefore, our responsibility, as people who measure problems and concerns in very different terms, to venture beyond our everyday anxieties and make something substantial of the privileged lives we have been born to?

> *The future is not a result of choices among alternative paths offered by the present, but a place that is created—created first in the mind and will, created next in activity. The future is not some place we are going to but one we are creating. The paths are not found, but made, and the activity of making them changes both the maker and the destination*
>
> **JOHN SCHAAR—FUTURIST**

A Pattern of Satisfaction

A proactive person takes care of life's foundations and then moves on to build something of substance. There's a pattern of satisfaction, a logical order to the gratification of our primitive needs, that leads us towards the inner conviction that we have unfulfilled potential. We progress towards the understanding that there must be something more to life, and this in turn creates in us the desire to accomplish more. In the late 1960s, humanistic psychologist, Abraham Maslow unveiled his now famous theory, known as *The Hierarchy of Needs*, which describes a predetermined pattern of satisfaction and a subsequent desire to move on to greater things.[30] This theory acknowledges that some of our needs take precedence over others. For example, our need to stay alive will preempt our concern for safety, or our basic need to belong to a community will usually take precedence over a desire to lead it.

Being Needs

Self-Actualization

Esteem Needs

Belonging Needs

Safety Needs

Physiological Needs

Deficit Needs

Deficit Needs

The first four layers of the needs pyramid deal with what Maslow described as deficit needs. If you lack any of these four basic requirements, you feel a profound need to acquire them. The consequences of leaving them unsatisfied could be disasterous, even life-threatening. However, once you have fulfilled these needs, you take their existance for granted. We crave what we lack, but once we get enough of it, the hunger stops. If they're taken care of, they are no longer needs that motivate us. Maslow classified these as basic survival needs and suggested that we are genetically coded to respond instinctively to these needs. As we progress through life, we move from one stage of needs to another, and once we have mastered our needs, we learn to balance them. However, in times of stress, or when we sense a threat to our survival, we may return our focus to previous needs. For example, a painful divorce could lead from a predominant focus on sense of worth (esteem needs), to a greater emphasis on the need to belong, to love and to be loved (belonging needs). Equally, if we fail to pay attention to the balance between our basic areas of need, we deny ourselves the possibility of growing to our full potential. If you are hungry, your focus will be food. If you are in danger, your focus will be caution. If you are unloved you will be anxious and lonely. If you lack self esteem, you will be living life on the defensive. There will be no room for growth.

- **Physiological Needs**

    These needs include the requirement for oxygen, water,

nourishment, sleep etc. As newborns, our world consists almost exclusively of physiological needs.

- **Safety Needs**
  Once you have taken care of your physiological needs, your focus turns to security and protection. You concentrate on your fears and anxieties and allay them by introducing structure and order into your life. You may be concerned about personal safety, or need to take steps to secure your financial future. If a society or culture feels threatened, or under attack, this level of need may take precedence, whatever level of progress has previously been made towards the fulfillment of higher needs.

- **The Need to Belong**
  As soon as your environment is safe, your thoughts are more likely to turn to the necessity to love and be loved. You will feel the need for fulfilling relationships with family, friends, colleagues and community. Our need to belong shows up throughout our lives as we choose partners, raise families, join clubs, become members of different commuinites, groups and organizations.

- **The Need for Esteem**
  Finally, we acknowledge our need for the respect of others, in the form of recognition, fame, appreciation or attention. We develop a sense of self-respect, recognizing our own level of competence, confidence and achievement. Of the

four levels, this will be the most difficult to achieve and the easiest to regress from.

Being Needs

The most important element of Maslow's theory is to be found at the tip of the pyramid. It is here that we encounter the concept of self-actualization, the motivation and ability to grow, or the needs associated with 'being'. Having taken care of our basic needs, we must now turn to a higher level of fulfillment. The needs that we associate with self-actualization are felt deeply and continuously. They are even likely to magnify as we feed them. These are the kind of needs that match our desire to fulfill our true potential, to recognize and live up to our responsibility to perform and progress. They reflect our duty to become our whole self and strive for the best that we can be. They represent the fullest, most vibrant and most effective version of ourselves. Those of us who succeed, do so because we've chosen to make a difference. You won't find successful people sitting on the sidelines. They've come to play and they're in the game. The winners glimpse the higher ground and set out to claim it. The *lifers* prefer to stay comfortably where they are and continue to focus on repetitive and introspective needs. Maslow identified a number of prominent people, whose lives he felt exemplified the higher level of achievement and self-actualization. Among them were people like Abraham Lincoln, Thomas Jefferson, Mahatma Gandhi, Albert Einstein and Eleanor Roosevelt. He also identified a number of qualities that self-actualized people like these have in common:

Grounded

These are people who can distinguish between hypocrisy and sincerity

Objective

They seek solutions to problems and don't take life's adversities personally

Present

Their focus is more closely fixed on the journey than the end goal

Independent

Self-actualizers rely on their own experiences and judgment and are comfortably self-sufficient

Compassionate

These people grow as a result of open and democratic values, social interest and humanity

Accepting

They take themselves and others as they are, valuing simplicity and spontaneity

Appreciative

Self-actualized people value the ordinary and have the ability to turn it into the extraordinary

After climbing a great hill, one only finds that there are many more hills to climb. I have taken a moment here to rest, to steal a view of the glorious vista that surrounds me, to look back on the distance I have come. But I can rest only for a moment , for with freedom comes responsibilities, and I dare not linger, for my long walk is not yet ended

NELSON MANDELA—FIRST BLACK SOUTH AFRICAN PRESIDENT

Kids Can Change the World

*J ust imagine if we all believed in ourselves and
worked together—young people, adults, seniors, all
cultures and all religions—all sharing our gifts and
talents…we have everything it takes*

CRAIG KIELBURGER—SPOKESPERSON FOR CHILDREN'S RIGHTS

Most of us are tired of being told that it takes a village to
raise a child. It's refreshing therefore to hear that Craig Kielburger believes it takes children to raise a village. And it's not
just empty rhetoric. He has spent a large part of his life proving
what a team of motivated kids can do. At the age of 12, Craig
came across the following front-page newspaper article
describing the murder of 12-year-old Iqbal Masih in Pakistan.

Battled Child Labour Boy, 12 Murdered

ISLAMABAD, Pakistan (AP) — When Iqbal Masih
was 4 years old, his parents sold him into slavery for less
than $16.

For the next six years, he remained shackled to a
carpet-weaving loom most of the time, tying tiny knots
hour after hour.

By the age of 12, he was free and travelling the
world in his crusade against the horrors of child labour.

On Sunday, Iqbal was shot dead while he and two
friends were riding their bikes in their village of
Muridke, 35 kilometres outside the eastern city of
Lahore. Some believe his murder was carried out by
angry members of the carpet industry who had made
repeated threats to silence the young activist.

Toronto Star, April 19, 1995

Craig was profoundly shocked by the gulf of difference that lay between the lives of two 12-year-old boys, one living in Pakistan and the other in Canada. Did he go to school and write an essay about it? Did he appease his conscience with a charitable donation? No, the teenager made the choice to take action. He shared this story with his brother Marc and with his schoolmates and motivated them to join him in making a difference. Together, they communicated the shocking reality of child labour to other groups of students and to the adult community. Together they founded an international organiza- tion, to liberate children from poverty, exploitation and abuse. They named it, *Free The Children*.

Where does a 12-year-old adolescent boy get the inner resolve to take on such a monumental task that has outpaced the collective wisdom of the world's most influential governing bodies? I doubt if he knew that he had it when he made his decision to take action. Both he and his classmates grew with the task and step by step developed an organization that "is dedicated to eliminating the exploitation of children around the world, by encouraging youth to volunteer in, as well as to create programs and activities that relieve the plight of under- privileged children."[31] Today *Free the Children* exists in more than 35 countries around the world and grows daily. Children under the age of 18 make all decisions regarding policy and the direction of the movement.

Since founding *Free the Children*, Craig has acted as a spokesperson for children's rights in more than 40 countries and has advocated on behalf of children in meetings with the world's political and religious leaders. Collectively, youth members of FTC have helped construct over 300 primary schools in rural areas of developing nations, providing education for over 15,000 children. They have distributed approximately 100,000 school information kits and in excess of 2.5 million dollars worth of medical supplies to needy families. At the time of writing, FTC supports portable water projects, health clinics, alternative income cooperatives and primary schools in 21 developing nations.

Despite the phenomenally compassionate contribution that this young man has made to society, he has always had to deal with a vocal group of detractors. At an early age he had to learn to deal with the heartache of being attacked publicly for his convictions. There were those who felt he was too young to be criticizing entire political systems. Some were outraged that a 12-year old should be dealing with sensitive subjects such as child prostitution. A Brazilian social worker asked, "Why is it that North Americans always think that they can save the world?" Despite the opposition, he remained undeterred. At a time that most adolescent boys are struggling to understand themselves, let alone their place in society, Craig continued to fight on behalf of the world's exploited children. In his book, *The Power of One*, he counters his critics with the suggestion that, "North Americans are not saving these children; we are supporting them in their struggle."

Young people continue to raise money for FTC projects via fundraising activities such as walk-a-thons or rock-a-thons, bake sales, raffles, selling their toys, doing odd jobs and services, organizing concerts and plays, collecting pop bottles and donating their birthday money. Craig Kielburger continues to donate the money he raises from speeches and awards, scholarships and book royalties. The extraordinary achievements that Craig and his brother have facilitated serve as an illustration to us all that it can be done, it has to be done, and that, although it will undoubtedly be difficult, it will also be infinitely rewarding.

Get Comfortable With Change

Change is uncomfortable but evolution is inevitable, because progress is something that wants to happen.[32] If you fear change you'll have difficulty making progress. And, if you don't recognize your responsibilities to make progress, you'll have a hard time being successful. I'll leave it to Barbie to expose you to the stark reality of life's mutations. When she first hit the shelves in 1959, the genetically improbable Barbie doll was aimed at 14-year-old teenagers. Scary as it may seem, the target age is now 4-year-old girls! Barbie, who was originally modeled on a quasi-pornographic Lilli doll from Germany, appears to conform to a pre-schooler's vision of beauty.[33] So there you have it: incontrovertible proof that the world is changing. Whether you call it progress or not is another matter entirely! When Barbie was born, the world population amounted to 3 billion, now it's 6.2 billion and in 2050, it's likely to become 9 billion (many of whom will probably own Barbie dolls). But we're not just experiencing tangible physical changes, we've also been making some spectacular mental shifts. It used to be said that the body of knowledge on this planet doubled somewhere around every 100 years. Nowadays, you can count on that happening about every two years. Today's leading companies have learned to anticipate the gathering speed of change, knowing that about half of what they know and do today will be obsolete within a matter of months! Internet data traffic is doubling every three to four months. If you think of an idea, you'd be wise to act quickly, because your competitors are inevitably closer than you think.

In their fascinating book, *Return on Imagination*, Tom Wujec and Sandra Muscat provide us with several clear illustrations of the speed at which we are confronted with change. "Thirty percent of 3M's revenues are from products less than four years old. Seventy-seven percent of Hewlett Packard's revenues are from products less than two years old. Eighty percent of Macromedia's revenues are from products less than one year old… In 1990 in the US, companies took an average of 35.5 months to bring products to market, but by 1995 companies were introducing new products on average every 23 months. By 2000 that had dropped to eleven months. Cars that took six years from concept to production in 1990 now take less than two years. Renault has stated that its goal is to produce a complete vehicle—from design to off the assembly line—in nine days."[34]

> *Change is the law of life and those who look only to the past or present are certain to miss the future*
>
> **JOHN F. KENNEDY**
> —35TH **PRESIDENT OF THE UNITED STATES**

We're living through a time that is driven by information and ingenuity. New data is being delivered to us so fast, that we're often having difficulty processing the ideas. We are building a brain-based New Economy on the twin pillars of technology and globalization. The most visible symbols of this new economic order are to be seen in the revolutions in computers, telecoms and the Internet. Not surprisingly, the new game is governed by a new set of rules and we all have to learn to become faster, more flexible and more innovative if we want the privilege of becoming, and remaining, a player. Increasingly, companies are driving responsibility down the line, empowering employees towards self-governance, decentralizing responsibility and making it the domain of the individual.[35] If you don't take the initiative, somebody's going to ask you to do it anyway. Domestically we're witnessing the effect of disruptive technology in our everyday lives, turning past perceptions and timeworn habits through 180°. Handheld digital assistants, digital cameras, MP3 Players, and the Internet all belong to the group of disruptive innovations that have blindsided us with their groundbreaking qualities and have entirely redefined the markets to which they belong. As consumers we are no longer impressed by the kind of incremental product improvements that promise us cleaner clothes, using marginally improved formulas. Frankly we won't be impressed until someone offers us clothes that clean themselves. However, just because we crave change doesn't mean we're comfortable with it.

*P*eople will suffer almost anything as long as it
means they don't have to change

DEEPAK CHOPRA, MD—HOLISTIC HEALER

Most of us are initially scared to death of change. It's far easier and far less stressful to keep things as they are. But, it's something we have to learn to deal with. Like most things in life, change is about choices. As Bob Proctor suggests, "Change is inevitable; personal growth is a choice." Not only is it possible for every last one of us to achieve success but it is also necessary. Change is going to happen, whether you like it or not and, either you can choose to let it pass you by or you can jump on and take control of the ride.

*O*nly I can change my life. No one else can do it for
me

CAROL BURNETT—COMEDIAN, ACTRESS, SINGER & DANCER

Your ability to anticipate, accept, manage and capitalize on change will determine your degree of success. We must constantly find ways of reinventing ourselves simply to maintain the status quo. If you're standing still, you're moving backwards. If, as we are told in Proverbs 13[17], progress wants to happen, we each have a responsibility to act as the catalyst. Are you experimenting? Are you challenging yourself? Do you use your imagination? Have you translated ideas into action? Are you living in the moment? Can you turn obstacles into opportunities? Are you learning anything new?

It's Time to Grow Up!

We've covered a lot of ground in the last few chapters and have acquired some new skills, insights and perspectives along the way. Now we need to do something with them. The simple difference between dreams and reality is action. What we've talked about is common sense and is readily absorbed and understood by most people. But, unless you can leverage the information by doing something about it, unless you can make use of your common sense, the advice remains entirely ineffective. The question is not, *can* you do it, but *will* you do it? And the answer is, YES YOU WILL, because you have to. Now is the time to turn newfound knowledge into action. Now is the time to make a commitment to yourself to do whatever it takes to achieve your goals. Individually and as a society, we're all too keen to lay blame elsewhere for our problems and our lack of achievement. At some stage in our lives we must all recognize our individual responsibility to become accountable for ourselves.

*I*n the old days, words like sin and Satan had a moral certitude. Today, they're replaced with self-help jargon, words like dysfunction and antisocial behavior, discouraging any responsibility for one's actions

DON HENLEY—SINGER/SONGWRITER

You have a dream and you know that it's possible to achieve it. Now you must recognize your responsibility to get on with it. Entrepreneur and educator, Robert Stuberg offers an insightful perspective on the bottom line of accountability when he suggests that, "The trouble with so many of us is that we underestimate the power of simplicity. We have a tendency, it seems, to over-complicate our lives and forget what's important and what's not. *We tend to mistake movement for achievement. We tend to focus on activities instead of results.* And as the pace of life continues to race along in the outside world, we forget that we have the power to control our lives regardless of what's going on outside."

We blame circumstance for our own dissatisfaction. I should know, I've done it myself. For too long, I blamed everything and everyone but myself for my own lack of fulfillment.

My mind-set included:

"Growing up fatherless must have left me with a permanent disadvantage and a collection of emotional scars".

"The misguided management philosophy of my employers is responsible for my lack of satisfaction at work".

"Unreasonable workloads and a long commute are forcing me to spend less time with my family".

"My schedule is so tight that I don't have time to see my friends, let alone learn any new skills"'

The night of my suburban epiphany, when I discovered the confidence to take responsibility for my own future, was the beginning of my journey towards self-actualization and personal accountability. I realized that the only way I was going to live up to the image of the person I aspired to be was to roll up my sleeves and become him. Having shared this momentous news with my dog Barkley out there in our local park, I then went home to start work on the rest of my life. My first step was to understand myself and my situation. My second was to become accountable and to make the choice and commitment to move forward. My third was to start my own business. Let's take a look at how my outlook has changed:

> *"Growing up father has taught me to be independent and to value the strength of a single parent. Growing up in a household of women has taught me to be a communicative and sensitive male!"*

> *"My own philosophy takes me in new directions every day. The more proactive I am with my business ventures, the more I seem to get in return. I am pursuing my passion with energy and enthusiasm. I love what I do".*

> *"Only I have the power to control the amount of time I spend with my family. It's my input that determines the outcome. I free up time to be with the people I love by maintaining a balance between my different life roles".*

> *"I'm never the victim of circumstance. My schedule is mine to organize as I wish and I strive to focus on quality of results rather than quantity of activities. I have renewed friendships, developed new skills and take a far more active role in the lives of my two daughters".*

Start at the Beginning

My dramatic change in circumstances was based on my simple decision to make a commitment. Again, it's amazing what power you unleash when you make a simple decision. In the space of a brief moment, a lifetime of hesitation and regret recedes and it's astounding how profoundly liberating that can be. I stopped blaming others for my own lack of action and realized that I had it in me to create the circumstances that would lead me to a better life. It dawned on me that I wanted this new life badly enough to take responsibility for it. No one else could do that for me, nor should they.

> *Even on the right track, you get run over if you just sit there*
>
> **WILL ROGERS—HUMOURIST & PHILANTHROPIST**

When I look back on the journey that I made, from who I was then to what I have become now, I can best describe my progress using 4 A's:

Awareness

Accountability

Action

Attitude

Awareness

Of the 4 A's, Awareness certainly takes the lion's share of the work. It's important to lay strong foundations for the actions that will follow. I began by taking stock of the person I was. I created a balance sheet of my assets and my liabilities, until I had a good set of illustrations to inform my self-perception. While I confronted my weaknesses, I also learnt that all was not lost, that my black hole wasn't going to last forever, and I became grateful for all the positive aspects of my life and my character.

I started opening my mind to the wealth of resources that could support me in my endeavour to change. While attending a seminar, I was introduced to a Lou Holtz video, entitled *Do Right*. It inspired me to discover more about the man, his advice, and how I could apply his brand of wisdom to my own life. I was also struck by the contents of a book called *The Right Mountain: Lessons from Everest on the Real Meaning of Success* by Jim Hayhurst. He talked about life-threatening experiences that affected team members. He described critical choices and lessons learned. It taught me how to define success for myself, on my own terms, both in my personal life and my career.

I was so struck by his message, which remained with me after finishing the book, that I contacted him and we spoke at length by phone. Jim put me in touch with a Career Transition Counsellor, who introduced me to more life-changing literature in the form of a book called *Do What You Are* by Paul D. Tieger and Barbara Barron-Tieger. The book encourages readers to *Discover the Perfect Career for You Through the Secrets of Personality Type.* Together my Career Counsellor and I explored the options that were open to me. It was as a result of this process that I became more aware of the reasons for my career unhappiness. I became conscious of what little effort I had been putting into my career in the broadcasting industry and, most importantly, I realized that searching for another job in that same industry would have been little more than changing deckchairs on the Titanic, it would only have been a lateral move. If I was going to save myself, I needed to do something completely different. This now clear to me, I needed to start my own business. While for many, self-employment might not have the appeal, or indeed might not be advisable, for me it was the only option. (Once again, identify the things that are good about what you do for a living and establish the route you will take to make them better.)

Despite my resolve, I still had reservations. Would I be able to take care of my family, pay my mortgage, my taxes and my living expenses? But like anything else, I found that progress starts with the initial step towards it. As my awareness grew, I became more confident that I was making the right move. I was more open to suggestion, started listening harder and increased my powers of observation. I grew better equipped to steer myself in the direction of the influences that were to be my salvation. I started focusing on relationships with real leaders. I'd known many people I'd describe as leaders, but my connections with them had only been superficial. I started examining my associations with these people, forcing myself to become better acquainted with their strengths, their successes and their values. Whether it was financial, professional, spiritual or personal, what did I admire about the success of these individuals? So many of my mentors have been extraordinarily generous with their time and their talents. I am so grateful to have had the opportunity to analyze success firsthand and determine how to emulate it.

One of my greatest business influences started his career in marketing with two blue-chip organizations and had the courage in 1981 to purchase an equal share in a small communications and promotions agency. 16 years later, he had turned his investment into a thriving multimillion-dollar event and conference company. He has been kind enough to share some of his profound insights with me and helped me avoid some of the mistakes I may have made if I'd been operating alone, by trial and error. As an individual, he exemplifies focus and determination and he simply refuses to lose. He has been living proof to me that, with the right attitude, anything can be done. He's an excellent networker and has demonstrated to me time and time again how beneficial networking can be. He is also a shining example of someone who understands his own strengths and has led me to examine mine.

In the arena of personal relationships, my wife is an inspiring example of balance, strength, perspective, selflessness and generosity of spirit. She continues to be a source of inspiration to me in every aspect of her successful outlook.

And two old acquaintances, who had been known to me when our paths occasionally crossed throughout my broadcasting career, have now become a larger part of my life through our common membership of a local fellowship. They have taught me so much about spiritual growth and the importance of helping others.

As I grew in my knowledge of myself and my understanding of the people I came into contact with, I started to take a fresh look at how I approached my relationships. Instead of always wondering what my association with someone else could do for me, I started wondering what benefit I could bring to a relationship. I also decided that, before I could move on, I needed to make amends for my past behaviour. I made a list of all the people that I believed I'd harmed or disappointed and I started my apologies. I liberated myself from the baggage I'd been carrying around, whether real or imaginary. I apologized in turn to my first wife, my employer, my current wife and my mother. It was extremely encouraging to discover that I still had their support, their encouragement and their energy behind me. Each of these people provided me with their counsel and guided me towards sources of inspiration that have stood the test of time. I explored *Tuesdays with Morrie*, by Mitch Albom, became familiar with, and bought into, the philosophies of Les Brown, Lou Holtz, Doug Wead, Tony Robbins and countless other inspirational figures. Today, I continue to learn from the experience and perspective of others.

Accountability

The second stage of my personal growth came when I recognized that acceptance does not equal permission. My newly discovered awareness had led to self-acceptance but it didn't give me permission to continue being that person. I had a responsibility to grow and develop. From that point in my life onwards, I have endeavoured to look at every situation I experience, every resentment I harbour, and establish what part I have played in events. In any situation, what I do determines what happens next.

Action

> *Ideas not coupled with action never become bigger than the brain cells they occupied*
>
> ARNOLD H. GLASOW

As a result of my increased awareness and my determination to become accountable, I resolved to take action on 3 major fronts:

1. **Accept responsibility for all the important elements of my life**

2. **Develop a plan of action and seek out people who could help with my transition**

3. **Take the Lou Holtz approach:**
   - *Do What's Right*
   - *Do The Best You Can*
   - *Treat Others the Way You Want to be Treated*

At a later stage of my journey of self-discovery, I came across the writings of Don Miguel Ruiz in his book of Toltec wisdom, entitled *The Four Agreements*.[36] This is a practical guide to personal transformation and freedom that echoed elements of the central message of earlier-mentioned influential voices that coincided with my turnaround. Don Miguel encourages us to break our old self-limiting agreements with life, in order to start practicing *The Four Agreements*:

1. **Be Impeccable With Your Word**
   Speak with integrity and use language positively and responsibly
2. **Don't Take Anything Personally**
   Avoid needless suffering by not over-reacting to the negative actions and opinions of others
3. **Don't Make Assumptions**
   Find the courage to ask questions and communicate clearly to avoid unhappy misunderstandings
4. **Always Do Your Best**
   Whatever your best is, do it and you will have no regrets

From the moment I made a commitment to take action, I couldn't believe how clear the path ahead became. The power of decision diminishes fear, so when I had decided to start my own business, I asked myself, " What's the worst thing that can happen?" When I recognized that the worst I could imagine was returning to work for someone else, I realized that I'd removed the fear. They say that when the student is ready the teacher will come and, from my own experience, I can honestly say that it's true. I suddenly had a clearer vision of what I needed to do and where I needed to turn for help to do it. I might as well have been walking around in a T-Shirt announcing my epiphany, because suddenly I seemed to be attracting interest from my entire network of contacts. There were people showing up to help me, without me even being aware of having asked for their assistance! It's incredible how magnetic commitment can be. When some enquired as to what I would do if my new career failed, my response was always: "Failure is not an option." Make your decision and you'll be in no doubt of your next step. But don't forget that commitment is a long-term deal. If you're going to achieve what you set out to do, you must dedicate yourself to continuous and coherent commitment. And you'd better be sure that the promise you've made reflects a deep-rooted passion and a sustainable set of values. We're all capable of the kind of instant commitment it takes to make a New Year's resolution but how many times have we lacked the level of dedication required to see us beyond the end of January?

*D**esire is the key to motivation, but it's determination and commitment to an unrelenting pursuit of your goal—a commitment to excellence—that will enable you to attain the success you seek*

MARIO ANDRETTI—GRAND PRIX LEGEND

I've come to learn that commitment makes all the difference between a life of abundance and a life of regret. And every time my commitment wavers (and it does), I rewind to that night in the park in order to reconnect with my vision of the future. And, whatever I'm working on, whatever situation I find myself in, whatever wall I'm up against, I 'Lou Holtz' it:

Am I doing what's right? Have I given it the best I can? Is this how I'd like to be treated?

Attitude

The journey that starts with self-awareness, progresses through the act of becoming accountable and finally takes off as we translate our thoughts into activity. However, all existing effort will have been wasted if we fail to cultivate a positive attitude. It's the keystone of the 4 A's and the subject of the first chapter in this book. We've already talked about it, so I won't dwell on the subject. Simply remember that future success has its origins in the mind. Positive thoughts produce successful, happy and fulfilled people. Learn to love what you do and don't be afraid to show it.

Responsibility: Run That By Me Again

- **Embrace your destiny**
  Nobody else has the ability to fulfill your unique purpose

- **Make a dent in the Universe**
  It's what you're here for

- **Check for the symptoms of affluenza**
  Along with privilege and comfort comes responsibility

- **Identify your pattern of satisfaction**
  Meet your basic requirements and move on

- **Climb to higher ground**
  Perform, progress and become your whole self

- **Get comfortable with change**
  If you don't dare to be different you won't make progress

- **Reinvent yourself**
  If Barbie can do it, so can you

- **Remember the 4 A's**
  Awareness, Accountability, Action, Attitude

- **Stop blaming other people**
  Create the circumstances that will lead to your dream

- **Make the commitment**
  Become accountable for yourself and do whatever it takes

- **Continue to take a personal inventory**
  Repeatedly check your attitude

- **Do something**
  The difference between dreams and reality is action

5

Deal With Difficulties

"Men wanted for hazardous journey.
Small wages. Bitter cold. Long months
of complete darkness. Constant danger.
Safe return doubtful. Honour and
recognition in case of success."
SIR ERNEST SHACKLETON, EXPLORER

Against the Odds

The quote you've just read was placed as a recruitment ad in London newspapers by British explorer, Sir Ernest Shackleton, when searching for candidates to join him on his 1914 expedition to the Antarctic. The advertisement, which could hardly be categorized as motivational, was a bold and courageous effort to get the Endurance Expedition moving. It was a starkly honest appraisal of how bitterly hard a polar expedition could be. It also carries a sweet reminder of the infinite rewards of success. No one's pretending for a moment that it will be easy to turn your dreams into reality, but most successful people will agree that the rewards are most definitely worth it.

Shackleton could easily have been discouraged and distracted by problems with benefactors, lack of public interest and challenges with ships and supplies, but instead he chose to focus his energies on finding the people who would constitute the lifeblood of this early 20th century polar adventure. If you placed such an ad today, you'd be lucky to get more than a handful of replies and you'd be likely to question the sanity of those who responded. In the early years of the last century, Sir Ernest's words attracted nearly 5,000 applicants to his British Imperial Trans-Antarctic Expedition. Shackleton is reported to have said, "It seemed as though all the men in Great Britain were determined to accompany me, the responses were so overwhelming."

As a result of those brief sentences in an English newspaper, Shackleton chose 27 men to accompany him on the first attempted crossing of the South Polar Continent from sea to sea. 1200 miles away from the nearest hint of civilization, with no means of communication and no hope of rescue, the words of that advertisement were to prove hauntingly accurate. For 10 months, the Endurance was immobilized by pack ice, which then destroyed the ship, prompted the expedition to abandon its initial goal of crossing the Antarctic, and forced these men instead to fight for survival for almost a year, in what must be the most inhospitable conditions on earth. It was his failure to achieve his goal as a polar explorer that led this ordinary man to discover something extraordinary within himself and the men in his protection. Against all the odds Shackleton kept 27 men alive, led every one of them to safety, frequently attempting and achieving the impossible. His 16-day, 800-

mile sea crossing in a lifeboat with six of his men, is considered by many to be the greatest open boat journey in history. His exhausting 17-mile journey in search of help, over the previously unscaled mountains and glaciers of South Georgia, was just the beginning of a series of additional challenges that stood between him and the rescue of his stranded men. It took three failed bids and 4 boats before he was finally able to return to the camp on Elephant Island to rescue the remaining members of his expedition. His story is arguably the greatest ever tale of human survival.

The level of difficulty that all of these men faced during that ill-fated expedition defies description. It far exceeded anything that they could have imagined, or any picture that Shackleton could have painted in a recruitment ad. But, as one nightmare replaced another, their leader, who was affectionately know as "The Boss", refused to accept the option of failure. When things didn't work out the way he planned, he redefined his goals. When survival was threatened, he tackled each obstacle in turn and resolutely refused to let any of his men die.

Despite falling short of his Antarctic dream, Shackleton recognized the spiritual success of the Endurance Expedition. Inspired by *Call of the Wild*, a poem by Robert W. Service, he wrote "We had 'suffered, starved and triumphed, grovelled down yet grasped at glory, grown bigger in the bigness of the whole.' We had seen God in His splendours, heard the text that Nature renders. We had reached the naked soul of man."[37] Sir Ernest Shackleton was described by his crew as "the greatest leader that ever came on God's earth, bar none." Unlike most other polar expeditions, every man under his command survived, not only in good health, but also in good spirits, due to Shackleton's extraordinary leadership skills. He attempted the impossible, failed only at the improbable and succeeded at the unimaginable.[38] He serves as an example to us all of how important it is to keep persevering, however hard it gets. It's certainly helped me to get my problems in perspective!

Shackleton once said, "I've often marvelled at the thin line that separates success from failure." And I say, "The problem with giving up is that you will never know how close you came to success."

Get Help

Relationships are all there is. Everything in the universe only exists because it is in relationship to everything else. Nothing exists in isolation. We have to stop pretending we are individuals that can go it alone

MARGARET J. WHEATLEY—LEADERSHIP CONSULTANT & SPEAKER

En route to your dream, you are going to encounter all kinds of obstacles. If you're like me, you may have spent a large part of your life steering carefully around anything that blocks your path. Eager to maintain the status quo, we've learned to compromise instead of confront and have often allowed ourselves to be diverted from our goals. Before we know where we are, we're heading down a side road to nowhere. Of course, there are situations where a head-on collision with an immovable object would not be wise. However, there are many more occasions when it's important to face up to whatever is in our way, clear the path and continue with the journey. Obstacles come in many shapes, forms and sizes:

People	Events
bad attitude *it may be yours, or someone else's but the biggest obstacle to progress is a bad attitude*	**difficult circumstances** *there will always be conditions that can cause problems but you're in charge of how you react*
lack of effort *you may lack the initiative to drive your dream, in which case you're sapping your own strength*	**lack of opportunity** *you may be seeing problems instead of potential but know that you have the power to create your own opportunities*
low energy *replace lethargy with vitality and you'll be capable of moving mountains*	**harsh reality** *life is tough and the sooner we face it, the sooner we start reaping the rewards*
no commitment *a lack of commitment to your dream will block the energy required to live it*	**unlucky coincidence** *bad things happen to good people but don't take it personally*
enthusiasm deficiency *the biggest roadblock you'll encounter is apathy*	**constant change** *change is uncomfortable, evolution is inevitable—embrace it*

The most important thing to understand when dealing with obstacles is that you're rarely going to be able to overcome them alone. Many of us are still locked in the pride-infested paradigm that persuades us we're weak if we seek help. That nagging little voice is telling us that we've failed to make the grade and that we should gracefully admit defeat. Pay no attention to the voice. Individual brilliance, creativity, energy and enthusiasm will go a long way towards defining your vision and launching your project, but you're going to need to call on the expertise and the skills of a whole village of people in order to achieve your ultimate goal. Few can achieve anything worthwhile alone. You need to be actively seeking out individuals who can make dreams happen. You need to be on the lookout for like-minded people with similar core values. You need to join forces and pool resources for mutual benefit. The synergies you create using the combined energies of a motivated team will far outweigh the effort you're going to have to make to aggregate, stimulate and coordinate its members.

As you assemble your band of helpers, be careful to stop yourself enlisting a team of yes people. Tempting as it is to surround yourself with folks who enthusiastically share your vision and applaud your inspiration, remember that you are looking for expertise, not praise. You're looking for a complementary team, not a collection of compliments. What you're searching for are people who can see beyond your horizons. Aim for balance among team members, so that their skills interleave to create a more valuable whole. Most people display distinct characteristics in their approach to any kind of collaborative work. There are many psychological profiling tests available to identify personality types. I've combined my favourites to give you a quick sketch of the four different profiles that work together to make up a well-adjusted team. Some people will display the characteristics of adjacent categories, although usually one will dominate. Others will clearly exhibit the characteristics of a single type:

Designers

These are the people who are known for their creativity. They're the ones that come up with the ideas that the rest of the team wish they'd thought of. They tend to think randomly, in concepts and abstracts and are invariably difficult to pin down. In a meeting or group environment, they'll probably spend more time moving around the room than sitting around a table. These are the people that take a wide-screen view of a situation from well outside traditional boundaries. They're full of bright, unconventional ideas and tend to break rules and act spontaneously. However, when it comes to implementation, they may act impulsively, quickly losing focus and moving on to apply their imagination elsewhere.

Developers

These are the planners, who love to take other people's ideas and work out what it will take to make them happen. Like the Designers, they don't mind breaking a few rules. They are clear thinkers, who have the ability to rise above the chaos created by an idea, take a birds eye view of the terrain and map out the way forward. They are the team's action figures who thrive on movement and achievement. Developers are high-energy, focused, fast-thinking strategists. However, they may lack the caution required to asses the viability of an idea and will rarely have the patience to deal with the day-to-day details of implementation.

Doubters

The Doubters know that not all ideas are good ones, and have assumed the responsibility of pointing out the pitfalls. Like the Designers, they are conceptual thinkers and their role is to challenge the validity of the ideas that the team generates. Doubters tend to be risk-averse and are experts at anticipating and avoiding problems before they arise. Like the Detailers, the Doubters are cautious and methodical and are always seeking ways to improve on existing concepts. However, if left unchecked, Doubters can often have a negative effect on the team and can become too focused on risk avoidance.

Detailers

The Detailers are the perfectionists who get hold of an idea when everyone else has finished with it. These are the organizers who deal with the day-to-day particulars of implementation, iron out all the inefficiencies, and stick with a project to see it through. They are the people who, given the rules and the requirements, will do everything necessary to turn a plan into reality. They're all about process and systems, and can only work in an ordered environment. Ask them to come up with a concept, and they're likely to be struck dumb with fear.

When you're choosing people to help you achieve your goals, remember to focus on a balance of skills. Try to marry highly creative and volatile contributors with pragmatic strategists and planners. Once the ideas crew becomes bored by its own brilliance and moves on to its next flight of fancy, the planners will march in and get very excited about directing operations. While optimism is a valuable commodity, every team needs its problem spotter; someone who can pick holes in creative ideas and anticipate problems before they have a chance of derailing an entire project. And remember to balance your conceptualists with a solid core of people who have spent their lives reading fine print. The sorters, sifters and processors of this world have an extremely valuable implementation role to play on your team. One man's meat is another man's poison. Find out what floats individual boats, take advantage of a variety of skills to achieve equilibrium, and make sure that the people helping you are focused on what they do best.

If you deal with every customer the same way, you will only close 25% to 30% of your contacts, because you will only close one personality type. But if you learn how to effectively work with all 4 personality types, you can conceivably close 100% of your contacts

ROD NICHOLS—NETWORK MARKETING CONSULTANT

Rediscover Your Network

We all have a network. Some of us just don't know where to look for it. Others haven't yet fully understood the extensive power of leverage. So much has been said and written about networks that you may have become disenchanted with the concept and you may be overlooking the essential message. However, I'm a strong believer in the power of networks, because they've always worked so well for me. If you identify and use your network properly, you'll be able to deal with any of the difficulties that threaten to destroy your dream because you'll always have people on hand to help you. Any good network is made up of several layers of contacts, which look something like this:

Close Contacts

These are your family connections and your closest friends: the people you know best and who probably know you better than anyone else.

Casual Contacts

These are the people who you know of through mutual acquaintances or as a result of brief encounters.

Coincidental Contacts

These links are the result of totally chance meetings, where you literally bump into someone who could be of great value to you.

Try to take advantage of your links with all the contacts you make, whatever category they fall under. Many people make the mistake of limiting their network to their closest contacts. The trouble with this is that you'll keep getting the same kind of help, which after a while will grow stale, and you'll start making the same kind of mistakes. Surprisingly, it's often your casual contacts who can provide you with the most beneficial help. They're not people that you get together with often, and you may not share common interests or experiences, but these are the people who can bring new perspective to your problems. They're not influenced by the history that you share with your close contacts; the sort of shared experiences that can get in the way of clarity. By reaching further into your network, you'll find yourself getting closer to your goal. Remember also that your networking skills will improve dramitically with practice, becasuse, as we all know, 'practice makes progress'. And, as you widen your web of contacts, get ready for the astonishing effects of serendipity. Be on the look out for the coincidental contact that will provide you with a shortcut to your dream. If you subscribe to US psychologist Stanley Milgram's 1960s small world theory, or if you've ever played the cult movie game, *The Six Degrees of Kevin Bacon*, you'll know that we're supposedly each separated by only six connections. Close, casual or coincidental, you're only six steps away from your dream.

Don't Talk to Strangers
Despite all the evidence that points to the power of networking, it seems to me that, whenever we hit a bump in the road and

need help, we so often turn to total strangers for assistance or advice. We're afraid of using our contacts for fear of being accused of impropriety. If we were being honest, it's really because we fear rejection. We're worried about appearing cap in hand, asking someone to make a charitable donation of time or talent. We don't want them to say no, nor do we want them to feel cornered or obliged to help out. So we take a Yellow Pages approach, without any point of reference, and start cold calling. We fail to understand the infinite power of referral.

In his book, *Dig Your Well Before You're Thirsty*, Harvey Mackay focuses on the power of networking. He argues that, "If I had to name the single characteristic shared by all the truly successful people I've met over a lifetime, I'd say it is the ability to create and nurture a network of contacts." He guarantees that if you learn to network properly, you'll never be more than a phone call away from a person in the position to help you get what you want, professionally, personally, financially or spiritually. If you're in need of a new dentist or a doctor, you'll almost certainly ask a friend, family member, or neighbour for a referral. You're unlikely to leave such an important choice to the chance pickings of the Yellow Pages. And in the majority of cases, those friends, family members and neighbours will be only too happy to pass on the information, because most of us instictively like to help out when we can.

During my sales training seminars, I often like to surprise attendees with a particularly graphic example of the energy that networking creates. Just as we're about to finish our first day of exercises, I ask everyone in the room to bring client contact details and cell phones with them the following day. I explain that I'm going to demonstrate the benefits of obtaining referrals versus cold calling, and that we're going to use their existing network of customer contacts to create a fresh list of prospects. At this point, the room usually falls deathly silent and the fear is palpable. You'd think that I'd just told them all that they only have 6 months to live. Shortly afterwards the objections gather momentum:

> *"I won't be able to get hold of my client list before tomorrow morning's session!"*
> *"I can't jeopardize important client relationships for the sake of a training exercise!"*
> *" I'm not going to embarrass my best clients by putting them on the spot!"*
> *"I don't want to appear cap-in-hand."*

Despite their overarching fear of rejection, most of them fall short of calling in sick the following day. When the exercise gets moving, invariably the most cynical members of the previous day's audience are the ones who obtain the most referrals, and who are the most enthusiastic about the benefits of the approach. Their initial fears have melted away. After all, what's the worst that could happen? A client could say no, or may not be able to think of a suitable referral. But, all is not lost. The relationship has not ended and the world continues to rotate. In all the years that I have been conducting this exercise we have only failed to achieve spectacular results on one occasion, when I was dealing with a particularly intransigent group of lawyers.

Otherwise, seminar delegates can't believe their good fortune when they build an impressive list of referrals as the result of an hour's worth of calls. They return to their lives with tangible proof that asking for referrals really works. In a room of 16 people involved in this one-hour exercise (that no one wants to do because it entails calling people out of the blue) the smallest number of referrals generated was 24 (the lawyers). The largest number so far has been a total of 2,453. The most typical result? Usually around 150 very valuable referrals.

But, don't just take my word for it. In a survey conducted for investment specialists, Nesbitt Burns, the company asked a sample of its clients whether they would give referrals if asked. 82% said yes. When asked if they had ever been approached for a referral, only 22% said they had. If you combine the power of referral with an effective selling process you're likely to close a sale in over 60% of cases. A cold call will generate a 5% success rate at best. And the technique can be applied to produce results in any area of your life; its success is not limited to a sales call. Recognize that other people want to help you. Whether you're seeking a recommendation, a referral, some advice, or a reference, recognize that the finest compliment you can pay someone is simply to ask for their advice. And, in many cases, your request for help will have more far reaching effects than you imagined. Once somone has given you advice, or granted you a favour, they often become caught up in your project and grow to be committed to your cause. Dr. Charles Dwyer is Director and Senior Research Analyst for the Management and Behavioral Science Center at The Wharton School. He has said that, "Asking for someone's advice is the most powerful way to positively influence that person, and once they offer their advice they become committed to its success." The power of networking is obviously worth considerably more than a wander through the Yellow Pages. When you enjoy a relationship with someone based on comfort and trust, they really do want to help you. Why not allow them to do so?

Ask Questions

I n life we are often wiser for questioning our answers than answering our questions

NOAH BEN SHEA—POET, PHILOSOPHER & SCHOLAR

Successful people do it all the time. They're constantly questioning the authenticity of the information they receive. Winners never assume that someone else knows what they're talking about just because they look good and appear confident. They don't believe everything they read, and frequently check sources of information. They're never afraid to ask a question, however stupid it may seem, and their more timid peers are usually grateful to them for pursuing clarity. They're eager to add to their own knowledge inventory by downloading information from the people they respect and admire. They actively seek out experts and grill them for information, so that they can constantly expand their own knowledge. When they encounter an obstacle, they find out *who* put it there, *why* it's causing a problem, *what* purpose it serves, *when* would be the right time to deal with it, *where* to turn for help and *how* to handle it.

I grew up in an education system that encouraged me to provide answers to questions that were already prepared for me by my teachers. When I didn't understand something, I assumed that it was my own fault, because I hadn't paid attention, or because I simply wasn't bright enough. I assumed that everybody else was in on the secret and that it was my responsibility to continue searching until I finally turned the right page. It didn't occur to me that I had the right to question what I was being taught. I was only partially aware of the opportunities I had to expand my educational horizon by simply asking the *right* questions. Too often, our emotional DNA, our social conditioning and our educational training have killed our curiosity. The problem is; if you're not curious, you're not learning. Curiosity never killed the cat; but a lack of it will turn you into a *lifer* and limit you to the great community of the also-rans! So many of the difficulties we face in life result from a lack of clarity. When confronted with an obstacle we often don't understand its significance, we're unsure of our next move. We don't know which way to turn. We're afraid to ask questions. We don't know how to find help.

I suggest you start with a single question. One question leads to another. Every answered question will increase your unique body of knowledge and feed your confidence. If you're faced with a problem that's preventing you from achieving your goal, try asking yourself some questions before you approach anyone else:

What did I do last time this problem came up?
Did it work, or was it a complete disaster?
What if I tried another approach?
What's the right thing to do?
Where can I find information that will help me?

Now, move on to seek the opinion of someone you value and trust. When you ask questions, it shows someone that you are interested and that you respect their opinion. People are flattered when you ask them questions because it shows that you care and that you value their input. Learn how to ask your questions, so that you will get the kind of answers you are looking for. Aim your questions at the right people, who possess the knowledge you need. Misdirected questions will lead to misdirected answers.

When you're in a group, make it your mission to be the one who's asking the questions. It's usually fear of other people's opinions that holds us back from firing off the questions we really want to ask when we're in a meeting, or find ourselves part of a group. Once you understand the infinite value of interrogation, the fear will be gone. Without questions, the content of a presentation or a meeting is limited and single-minded. As soon as you start asking questions, the group starts to communicate, ideas begin to interconnect, minds start to focus and problems seem to disappear. The meeting becomes a basis for discussion instead of an end in itself.

Be Prepared to Persevere

There are no short cuts to any place worth going
BEVERLY SILLS—OPERA SINGER

Beyond every inspiration there lies a great deal of contemplation, preparation, perspiration, and determination. We have to be prepared to put in the effort, energy and enthusiasm it takes to achieve a worthwhile objective. And we have to be ready to deal with the obstructions and frustrations that we will inevitably encounter along the way. There'll be research that needs doing, plans that need writing, skills that need learning, collaborators who need persuading, finance that needs raising, doubters who need motivating, objections that need overcoming and circumstances that need altering. We have to understand that there will be peaks and there will be valleys, and we have to learn how to sustain ourselves through the valleys, because the view from the mountain is worth it. I once heard Les Brown say, "A setback is a setup for a comeback." Difficulty is often what drives us closer to our goals. We gain strength through adversity and become better people when we are forced to face up to our challenges. Skill, brains, talent and virtue are nothing without perseverance.

You don't drown by falling in the water; you drown by staying there
EDWIN LOUIS COLE—FOUNDER OF THE CHRISTIAN MEN'S NETWORK

Take It From Tommy

Wealthy, self-made American hero, Thomas Alva Edison was an eclectic entrepreneur who is now known to us as one of the world's greatest inventors. Entire industries have been founded on the strength of his discoveries, many of which have been responsible for revolutionizing daily life. His name is so closely associated with the light bulb that many people are unaware that his prolific talents were also linked to other success stories, such as the invention of the phonograph, the development of early motion pictures and improvements to the telegraph. In fact, throughout his career, Edison held a total of 1,093 separate patents, including patent # 248431 for preserving fruit! As a boy, Thomas only managed 3 months of school before being unceremoniously kicked out. His teacher saw him as a disruptive influence with a mind that was incapable of staying on topic. Luckily, Tom's Mom was made of stronger stuff and, with unquenchable faith in her son, took it upon herself to homeschool him!

Known for his outstanding successes, Edison was no stranger to the extremes of hard work and failure. Fascinated by cement, he founded the Edison Portland Cement Co. in 1899 and set out to manufacture cement phonograph cabinets, pianos, houses and Yankee Stadium. Although his concrete legacy lives on in the Bronx, the cement pianos never really caught on. But this was a guy who never gave up. Take the light bulb as an example. It's said that Edison failed over 6,000 times before perfecting the first electric light bulb. But, because he believed that there was an alternative to gas light, Edison refused to give up. Asked by a journalist why he insisted in believing that he could use electricity to produce light when it was obvious that gas lights were here to stay, Edison replied, "Young man, don't you realize that I have not failed but have succcessfully discovered six thousand ways that won't work!" As far as he was concerned, every failure brought him closer to success.

The best way to escape from a problem is to solve it
ALAN SAPORTA—MUSICIAN

He was relentless in his search for materials that would produce the perfect filament. He sent people to China, Japan, South America, Asia, Jamaica, Ceylon and Burma to search for fibres to test in his laboratory, and none of them worked. For thirteen months he repeated one failure after another. And finally, on October 21, 1879, it occurred to him to try using a carbonized cotton fibre. After exhausting two spools of cotton, he produced the perfect strand, which promptly broke when he tried to place it in the glass tube. Undeterred, he worked through the next two days and nights without a break until he succeeded in placing a carbonized thread into a vacuum-sealed bulb. Which turned out to be a very bright idea!

Nobody's a natural. You work hard to get good and then work to get better
PAUL COFFEY—NHL PLAYER

Remember Rocky Balboa?

Sylvester Stallone has achieved international recognition as an actor, writer and director since *Rocky* hit the screens back in 1976. But it wasn't always that way. Leaving college before graduation, Stallone had gone to New York City in search of an acting career. By 1973, he'd auditioned for nearly all the casting agents in the city and attended thousands of acting calls, with minimal success. While waiting for his lucky break, Stallone began writing screenplays and landed a role in his first movie in 1974. With the money he earned, Sylvester headed for Hollywood, where he managed to get a few small TV and movie roles. He also continued writing.

Down to his last $100, with 32 rejected scripts to his name and thoroughly discouraged by his lack of success, Stallone was inspired by a little-known New Jersey club boxer named Chuck Wepner. Known as the "Bayonne Bleeder", the fighter had challenged Muhammad Ali in a heavyweight title bout in Ohio and managed to last 15 rounds, knocking Ali down in the process. Stallone seized the concept, and within three days had turned it into the first draft of a screenplay. A studio picked up on it and offered Stallone $20,000 for his script, suggesting Robert Redford, Ryan O'Neal, Burt Reynolds or James Caan in the title role. By this time, Stallone was already displaying the gutsy, optimistic perseverance of the movie's main character and decided to go for the million to one shot. He wanted to play the lead and he even offered to do it for free. When they declined his offer, he refused to hand over the script and they increased their bid to $80,000 if he'd drop the idea of playing Rocky. Faced with Stallone's increasing intransigence, they told him he'd get $200,000, if he'd let Redford do it. They eventually increased their offer to $330,000, but it made no difference to Stallone. He'd decided on an all or nothing deal and was prepared to stick by it.

*P**roblems are only opportunities in work clothes*
HENRY KAISER—GUITARIST

Finally, the studio caved and gave him the lead. They paid him the $20,000 they'd agreed for the script plus $340 per week to act. His net income from the final deal was only $6,000 once he'd paid his agent, the taxman and his expenses. The movie was made in 28 days, at a cost of $1 million. It grossed over $100 million, was nominated for 10 Academy Awards, won 3, and spawned 4 more Rocky movies, grossing almost $1 billion. And, as we all now know, Sylvester Stallone's stubborn persistence turned him into an international movie star.

…It is only by working with an energy which is almost superhuman and which looks to uninterested spectators like insanity that we can accomplish anything worth the achievement…

WOODROW WILSON
—28TH PRESIDENT OF THE UNITED STATES

Prioritize Your Problems

The problem with problems is that they always seem to hunt in packs. It never rains but it pours and, as the difficulties, predicaments, fears, objections, uncertainties, conflicts, dilemmas and self-ridicule pile up, we often become so intimidated that we give up way before we reach our intended goal. Sometimes the obstacles look so big and unfriendly that we can barely see daylight on the other side and we simply don't have the courage to continue. Which is why we should take things one step at a time. Don't try to overcome all of your obstacles in a single sweep. A problem lacks the bravado of a bully when it's confronted alone. If you identify your problems, give them a personality and separate them from their friends, you'll find that, individually, they're not so tough after all. Deal with them one at a time and you'll find that each victory gives you the courage to move on to the next confrontation. It's often the conflicts that you fear the most that turn out to respond to the simplest of solutions.

> *N**ever try to solve all the problems at once—make them line up for you one-by-one*
>
> **RICHARD SLOMA—ATTORNEY & AUTHOR**

Try to be brave enough to do the things you don't want to do. Faced with a daily 'to do list', we're all tempted to tackle the simplest and the most enjoyable tasks. Dealing with the no-brainers helps us to feel like we're actually achieving something without wasting too much energy, going through too much hassle, or making too many enemies. The problem with this approach, is that the unpleasant jobs start to pile up and, before we know where we are, we're face to face with a big, daunting, audacious obstacle. Learn to deal with the problems you'd prefer to avoid, by bringing them to the top of your list. One by one, your achievements will accumulate to the point that they overshadow any obstacles that come your way.

> *I*t was high counsel that I once heard given to a young person, 'Always do what you are afraid to do'
>
> **RALPH WALDO EMERSON—AUTHOR, POET & PHILOSOPHER**

Make Your Objective the Centre of Attention

In the words of Stephen Covey, "The main thing is to keep the main thing the main thing." However tough the going gets, try to remember why the hell you're doing whatever it is that you're doing in the first place. Don't let that objective out of your sight. Pin it down, hold on tight and don't, whatever you do, let go.

I know it can be so easy to get sidetracked. It's happened to all of us in one meeting or another. We're there to help move a project forward and, before we know it, we're all raising objections, discussing the details of every possible pitfall and looking to the past for examples of similarly doomed missions. Halfway through the meeting most people have lost their way, forgetting why they came in the first place. Everybody leaves with a fragmented picture of what needs to be done next. They're all following different paths, and not one leads to the original destination. If you want to avoid such an outcome, always be sure to maintain a clear focus on your objective. Pamper it, parade it and proclaim it, until everyone shares a common vision and all individual actions relate to the ultimate goal.

Doug Wead gives us a wonderful example of the power of focus when he talks of the legendary story of David and Goliath. As we all know, Goliath was the larger-than-life obstacle to David's dreams. Or so it seemed. When he first heard him speak, David was so overwhelmed by Goliath's strength and stature that he fled, along with all of Israel! As it turned out, Goliath was probably the best thing that ever happened to David. Back at the campfires, young David finds out that the reward for killing Goliath is to become a prince, marry the princess, ride a fine horse and get a huge tax break. Suddenly, David understands the benefits of overcoming the obstacle. He has a clear objective in mind (marry princess) and everything he does from this point onward is aimed at clearing the obstacles (whatever their size) from his path. Armed with a purpose, this nobody shepherd succeeded in focusing on the princess, not the problem, and came home with all the prizes. He didn't dwell on Goliath's obvious height advantage, superior strength or past prowess. He simply imagined himself on the horse, with the girl and the money. With his eye firmly on the prize, David went out and killed himself a giant Philistine, and Bath Sheba became his bride.

*I*n life you'll always be faced with a series of god-ordained opportunities brilliantly disguised as problems and challenges

CHARLES UDALL—DEVELOPMENT ENGINEER

Difficulties: Run That By Me Again

- **Understand that there are no free lunches**
  If it's plain sailing, you probably haven't left harbour

- **Pay for your progress**
  The steeper the climb, the more breathtaking the view

- **Get help**
  It takes a village to reach a goal

- **Balance your team**
  Offset your own weakness with someone else's strength

- **Use your connections**
  Widen your web of contacts

- **Allow people to help you**
  They love to be of assistance

- **Be inquisitive**
  The most successful people ask the most questions

- **Don't assume**
  Make it your business to interpret correctly

- **Never give up**
  Remember, "A setback is a setup for a comeback"

- **Take one step at a time**
  Each victory provides courage for the next confrontation

- **Do what you don't want to do**
  Someone's got to do the dirty work

- **Remember the main thing**
  Don't let your objective wander out of sight

6

Become A Progressive Leader

"A leader is one who knows the way,
goes the way and shows the way."

JOHN C. MAXWELL, INJOY GROUP FOUNDER

Leadership Material

There are those who believe that leaders are born, not made. That sounds to me like a cast iron excuse for behaving like a sheep. Pay little attention to this line of thinking, because there is undoubtedly the potential for leadership in all of us and, just like anything else in life, leadership can be learned. There are plenty of mentors out there, waiting for eager apprentices to appear. While some of us may exit the womb screaming, ready for action, with the words "person in charge" prominently tattooed on a body part, there are others who put lifelong time and effort into studying, practising and assuming the skills of leadership. The problem with so many of us is that we don't think we house the potential to inspire others. As usual, I blame the paradigm, which in this case has us believing that all leaders must be bold and brazen. I grew up thinking that the heroes of this world are always the loudest, strongest, fiercest, most daring of adventurers. The dashing leaders of my dreams would invariably emerge triumphantly, the conquering hero, or sit proudly on horseback at the brow of a hill. From their superior vantage point, they would search the horizon for signs of greatness, with a presence that was never the slightest bit short of commanding. At some point in their illustrious careers, these chosen few would inevitably be called upon to 'eliminate' someone (but maybe that's just a boy thing), or at least inflict some kind of permanent damage. This would be their measure of toughness and steely determination, as well as their commitment to be true to a higher purpose.

It was the same at school. The kids who we all thought of as leaders would be the ones we feared the most. They were the students who always got to pick their teams, who headed up the cliques and the committees, and who walked the halls with a predictable air of celebrity and ownership. We equated tyranny with supremacy, and failed to understand the potential for informed and responsible leadership that lay dormant within all of us followers.

Thankfully, the command and control style of leadership that many of us absorbed from TV, books and movies has gradually made way for a new, gentler, kinder design of stewardship, which increasingly casts the leader in the role of servant. The enlightened leader understands the importance of loyalty and integrity and has learned to balance strength with humanity.

A progressive leader will aim to simplify and demystify and will, at all cost, avoid the encyclopedic jargon of ivory towers. Independent learners, with strong beliefs and values that they articulate and act upon, these people understand the privilege and responsibility of their position. Never willing to assume anything, today's successful leaders have the courage to challenge accepted wisdom, and the vision to do things differently. Many of the friends I admire most for their leadership qualities today never stood out from the crowd back in their school days. Like all good learners, the best leaders have grown into their roles. And, while many admirable motivators have impressed us with their brilliance, super intelligence is not a prerequisite for effective leadership. Proverbial wisdom tells us that fortune favours the brave, and personally, I would rate courage higher on my list of desirable leadership qualities. Of course there are plenty of different perspectives and many more elements that make up the leadership mix. What follows is my idea of the ingredients that combine to produce today's enlightened hero or heroine.

Servant Leadership

If you wish to be a leader you will be frustrated, for very few people wish to be led. If you aim to be a servant you will never be frustrated

FRANK F. WARREN
—PRESIDENT OF WHITWORTH COLLEGE 1940–1963

It seems that Ernest Shackleton is the 'new black'! Fashionable in a way that he never was in his own lifetime, everybody's talking about the man, making movies about him, writing books from every possible perspective, and filling newspapers with the latest take on his heroic exploits. At the risk of repeating myself (and others), I feel compelled to add my voice to the swelling numbers and borrow his Antarctic experience once again; this time to illustrate what seems to me to be the very essence of successful leadership.

Our traditional leadership models have tended to focus on the elevated status of a single individual and have centred almost exclusively on the power of command and control. We have been fed a diet of groundbreaking, flag-waving, do-as-I-say politicians and belligerent warriors, inciting the masses to play follow-the-leader, without ever questioning the route or the method of transport. Shackleton broke that mould way ahead of his time, displaying a considerable talent for what we now refer to as servant leadership.

Sir Ernest lived during a macho era of rugged explorers and British Imperialism. During the early years of The House of Windsor, the British public measured success in terms of territorial gains and degrees of heroic suffering. Winning was the ultimate measure of success, self-sacrifice was revered, and the more tragic the hero, the better. The hierarchical, and often hypocritical, society of post-Victorian Britain was strictly ordered by class and custom. Shackleton evidently saw things differently. Success in Shackleton terms became measured in terms of survival, not flag-planting. And, as for leadership, he broke every rule in the turn-of-the-century book. The man was part rugged explorer and part Florence Nightingale; a Viking with a mother's heart, as a friend once described him.[39] He ran an egalitarian expedition, led by example, and valued the individual contributions of every man in his keeping.

During his Polar Expeditions, Shackleton earned the respect of his men and a reputation for putting the mental and physical well being of his teams above all else, including himself. Although he was perfectly capable of taking control where necessary, he knew that the key to successful leadership lay in winning hearts and minds. He knew that survival was as much about a spiritual struggle as it was about physical combat.

Shackleton maintained the respect of his men by showing equal respect for their opinions and contributions:

- When the Endurance became lodged in pack ice, Shackleton worked with his men to pursue every possible means of extricating the ship. Although he knew these attempts would be futile, he wanted every man to understand for himself why the expedition would have to wait out the winter in the ice. He wanted to avoid the divisive effects of second-guessing.

Shackleton's Antarctic team remained cohesive and positive because he kept them equal:

- He ignored the rigid class system of the time and had scientists scrubbing floors alongside seamen; university professors eating beside Yorkshire fishermen.

Shackleton listened to each member of his team, and played to the strengths of the individual. In turn he empowered them to contribute to their collective survival:

- Captain Frank Worsley's exceptional navigation guided the men to Elephant and South Georgia Islands
- Carpenter Chippy McNeish reinforced the lifeboats
- Cook Charles Green created meals day after day with severely limited resources
- Doctors Macklin and McIlroy saved steward Perce Blackborrow from gangrene
- Second-in-command Frank Wild led the 21 men on Elephant Island after Shackleton's small rescue operation departed for South Georgia

Shackleton frequently put the needs of his men before his own and made sure that he and his officers did not receive preferential treatment:

- When drawing lots for sleeping bags, somehow Shackleton and his fellow officers consistently ended up with the wool ones and all the warm fur bags went to the men under them.
- To help his men get over the trauma of having to abandon the Endurance, Shackleton rose early in the morning, made hot milk, and hand-delivered it to every tent in the camp.
- During the 17-day journey to South Georgia in the open lifeboat *James Caird*, Shackleton constantly monitored the health of his companions. Captain Frank Worsley wrote, "Whenever Shackleton notices that a man seems extra cold and shivering, he immediately orders another hot drink served to all." Worsley explained that Shackleton was careful not to single out the man suffering the most, because he would not want to frighten him about his condition.

Shackleton led by example and his humanitarian approach was
infectious:

- When First Officer Lionel Greenstreet spilled his much-
  needed milk on the ice, the seven men who shared his tent
  silently poured some of their equally precious ration into
  his mug, refilling it.[40]

> *W*hosoever will be chief among you, let him be
> *your servant*
>
> NEW TESTAMENT—MATTHEW 20:27

Gandhi exemplified servant leadership, as did Mother
Teresa. Both Eleanor Roosevelt and Dr. Martin Luther King
had a gift for it. Nelson Mandela is a classic current day
example and, more recently, Rudy Giuliani, who displayed the
sensitive compassion of a leader in the service of his New York
constituents, when dealing with the overwhelming consequences of 9/11. Gradually, throughout the 20th Century, with
the help of people like Shackleton, Gandhi and Mandela, our
definition of what makes an outstanding leader has evolved to
be less concerned with unilaterally defining the direction of the
group, and more to do with listening to what people want and
making it happen for them. Consider this reflection from
TIME magazine:

> *"For having more faith in us than we had in ourselves, for*
> *being brave when required and rude where appropriate*
> *and tender without being trite, for not sleeping and not*
> *quitting and not shrinking from the pain all around him,*

Rudy Giuliani, Mayor of the World, is TIME 2001 Person of the Year."

A more inclusive, communicative form of inspirational guidance has now largely replaced the once formal and hierarchical approach that was often applied to matters of leadership. We can all learn to lead by serving others:

- **Define** and articulate the vision that will inspire your team
- **Set the goals** that will describe your mutual achievement
- **Make resources available** to empower your group
- **Anticipate problems** and learn to see around corners
- **Remove roadblocks** impeding your collective success
- **Act as group translator**, interpreter and simplifier
- **Maintain the clear focus** of your shared mission
- **Show relentless optimism** for the communal dream
- **Motivate by example** and empathize by the truck load
- **Demonstrate loyalty** and integrity
- **Sustain**, encourage, guide, train and discipline

*E*verybody can be great... because anybody can serve. You don't have to have a college degree to serve. You don't have to make your subject and verb agree to serve. You only need a heart full of grace. A soul generated by love*

MARTIN LUTHER KING JR.—STATESMAN

I believe Lou Holtz summed up the concept of servant leadership best when he suggested that everything in life and everything in business is about helping other people get what they want. Let me remind you of the three basic rules that govern his philosophy:

- **Do What's Right**
- **Do Your Best** (commit to excellence in all you do)
- **Treat Others The Way You Want to be Treated**

If Lou Holtz were analyzing a person's leadership qualities, he'd be asking:

- **Can I Trust You?**
- **Are You Committed to Excellence?**
- **Do You Care About Me?**

Not Everyone Likes You

Being responsible sometimes means pissing people off
GENERAL COLIN POWELL—US SECRETARY OF STATE

If you're going to be a leader, you can't be everybody's friend. And that's a hard thing to come to terms with because, however thick-skinned we may be, instinctively we all like to be liked. Shackleton's leadership style, as inclusive, warm and familial as it may have seemed, involved its fair share of unpopular decision-making. On their safe return from the Antarctic, all members of Shackleton's expedition were awarded Polar Medals by King

George V. Shackleton, however, withheld these medals from six of his men, who he felt had not merited the distinction. Talk about a tough call!

As a leader, you'll be responsible for the collective success of a group of people, whether they're putting together a bake sale, or responsible for the future of an entire nation. It's a role that unavoidably entails tough choices and impactful decision-making. If you want to be a leader, you can't sit on the fence. While there is certainly, and always, a place for diplomacy, actions have consequences and you'll never make any progress if you try to please everyone. You won't define your leadership style by clinging to the comfort of middle ground. If you're constantly playing the conciliator, mediating conflict and gently smoothing ruffled feathers, you're probably facilitating someone else's ascent to success. You won't be promoting your own interests, nor will you be championing the collective cause. Your lack of strength and resolve could be driving away the most valuable members of your team, as frustration builds. You must learn to be courageous, because, if we're not prepared to make tough decisions, and a few enemies on the way, the best we can aspire to is mediocrity. We have to be prepared to forsake our comfort zones and stride out to the very edge. The view from there may prove to be profoundly disappointing, or utterly breathtaking. That's the risk you take. But a single spectacular vista is worth a fistful of disappointments.

If we're going to excel, there are people that we need to confront. And we should start with ourselves; our own attitudes, prejudices and insecurities. Then we must learn to find the courage to confront our adversaries. People may badmouth our efforts, our policies and our personalities as a result of strongly held beliefs that conflict with our own opinions. But don't allow confrontation to steer you away from your goals. Recognize that the best way to deal with detractors is through clear communication. When someone understands your point of view, and you, in turn understand the opposing perspective, you will often be able to join forces and create valuable synergies in the process. Welcome the people that question your abilities, encourage diversity of outlook and opinion, and actively seek out people who are smarter, quicker and more insightful than you are. They will be valuable assets on the team that's going to lead you to your dream.

Shut Up & Listen

The older I grow the more I listen to people who don't talk much

GERMAIN G. GLIEN—AUTHOR

My friends are never short of advice. One of the more popular directives, which I think is borrowed from the handbook of Stoic philosophy, has frequently been suggested to me and goes something like this: "We were given two ears and only one mouth for a good reason. We need to listen twice as much as we speak." A good leader needs to be a clear communicator, but that doesn't mean doing all the talking. The most instructive portion of any communication is the time spent listening.

A rousing speech can be just what the doctor ordered to boost flagging morale and raise dejected spirits but if the text is misdirected, the message will be lost and the problems will remain unsolved. Leaders learn to listen. As a leader, you have to know your audience, because unless you've grasped the 360° view, you won't be able to provide effective guidance.

I'm a showman by nature, and love performing in front of a crowd. Consequently, I find it hard to keep quiet. With the help of my friends, family and colleagues, I'm trying to pause frequently for breath, and listen to what it is that people really want. I'm also teaching myself to pay attention when I'm listening. It's one thing to keep quiet, quite another to absorb the details of another person's conversation; yet another to understand and act upon them. And, when I really concentrate on making effective communication a true priority, I also understand that not all the signals I get from other people will be verbal. I'm learning to listen to a mixture of signs that will help me absorb another person's perspective. Actions speak louder than words, and so does body language. Learn to look for the signals and know how to react to them.

Lead By Example

The actions of a responsible executive are contagious
JOE BATTON—'DEAN OF AMERICAN SALES TRAINERS'

Most human beings are accomplished mimics, learning by the monkey-see-monkey-do method. Whether you're parenting, providing a community service, or steering a multinational, it's your attitude, behaviour and actions that describe the culture surrounding you. Your style becomes the model for the people you serve. Whatever your approach, it will be contagious, so you'd better make sure that it's not toxic. I've known too many people who are very good at creating emotional toxins, and I've watched the poison they produce spread like wildfire throughout an organization. The higher someone ranks in an association, the greater the toxic effect. A contaminated CEO will infect an entire company.[41] Luckily, the reverse is also true. Qualities like integrity, loyalty, honesty, empathy, tolerance, compassion, courage, clarity, energy, enthusiasm, optimism and humility rub off on those that witness them, and will rapidly permeate the culture of an organization.

In any organization or enterprise, whether it's a business, a school, a community service, a government, a charity, or any other, it is paramount to remember that the people in the group are its most valuable asset. Too bad that so many of us fail to recognize the immense value of the people who surround us. The leader who understands the power of people and treats them as an asset, instead of an impediment, has also understood the power that one person has to positively influence another. By putting people first, before the money, before the time efficiencies, before the statistics, a leader becomes a winner and creates an environment that nurtures enlightened and positive growth. The profits, the time efficiencies and the positive statistics will naturally flow when people are happy, understood and fulfilled. The leader who submerges ego in favour of equality leads by positive example. The leader who combines integrity with effort, energy and enthusiasm in all aspects of governance will emerge as a clear role model, and become known as an individual whose initiatives resonate with success.

Keep Your Eye on the Details

A *lways sweat the small stuff*

RUDOLPH W. GIULIANI—*TIME* 2001 PERSON OF THE YEAR

Our MBA-driven business world encourages us to obsess about becoming strategists, and to be wary of the myopic tacticians who will attempt to plague us all with their micromanagement techniques. Richard Carlson begs us not to sweat the small stuff. I beg to differ. I think we're so busy focusing on the big picture that we've lost sight of the small steps that are going to get us there. Lately I've seen too many people taking in the view from a ten thousand-foot vantage point, when they should really be zooming in for a close-up. In doing so they'd at least be able to witness the chaos they're causing! If you confine yourself to the bigger picture, and don't inform yourself of the detail, you won't be accountable for your enterprise. And, if you're not accountable, you're not a true leader. An inspired idea or a dazzling vision loses its sheen if it's impractical and impossible to implement. US Secretary of State, Colin Powell, believes that, "Good leaders delegate and empower others liberally, but they pay attention to details, every day."[42] It's so often the small things that we ignore every day that become the biggest drain on our energy. It's the tasks that we fail to complete that cause the clutter in our lives and lead to the repetition that plagues the *lifers*. The photos that you never put in the album, the missing button that you haven't replaced, the desk that you didn't have time to tidy, the birthday present that you forgot to send. If you want to create good energy, Feng Shui, the latest in architectural acupuncture, will counsel you to eliminate clutter. Tidy up the small issues in your life and you'll create space for something of far greater importance. So long as we don't become detail-obsessed, and so long as we're always checking and challenging the wisdom of the details we're dealing with, a close focus can be a good thing. This thinking is exemplified by the actions of New York's ex-mayor, Giuliani. The individual who emerged as a clear leader in the wake of the New York terrorist attacks, believes that when you pay close attention to the small stuff, you set the right tone for the bigger stuff. By homing in on the detail, you can stop minor issues from spiraling into major disasters. And, when major disasters do strike out of the blue (as they inevitably will), your detailed knowledge is primed to help you to decide how to clean up.[43]

People who sweat the small stuff generally subscribe to the *Broken Windows Theory*,[44] as described by criminologists George Kelling and James Q. Wilson. They hold that a broken window left unrepaired suggests a lack of care for the building, and invites further vandalism. Untended, property becomes fair game for petty criminals, as well as people who ordinarily would not dream of behaving unlawfully. Furthermore the authors contend that if, or when, disorderly behaviour is left unchecked, the message sent is that nobody cares about the community, and this leads to more serious disorder and crime. If you subscribe to the wisdom of the theory, the solution, it seems, is to get tough on minor issues, in order to reduce the incidence of major ones.

In 1994, William Bratton became the top cop in New York City, under Rudy Giuliani's administration. Together they used the *Broken Windows Theory* to clean up crime in the city. The success of their approach has been well-documented, but they certainly also faced a significant number of challenges throughout the practical execution of their plan. However, during Bratton's two-year tenure there was a 39% drop in crime and a 50% reduction in murders. When police in New York began to focus on petty crimes, they found that many of the people caught for minor offences had links to more serious crimes. By starting with the details, and sweating through the small stuff, they were able set the tone for the wider landscape, and the streets of New York became considerably safer.

Aim To Excel

*W*hatever you are, be a good one

ABRAHAM LINCOLN

—16TH **PRESIDENT OF THE UNITED STATES**

To be an effective leader, you must be excellent at what you do, and not afraid to demonstrate it with humility:

Excellent Leaders Never Assume

A friend of mine displays a large banner in his office, instructing himself, and anyone else who wanders in there, to "ASSUME NOTHING." It is a mantra that he repeats endlessly. It is a theme that permeates every formal meeting or casual encounter he has with his colleagues and staff. It is a belief that he carries into his personal life. He excels at asking questions, striking directly at the heart of any matter that ignites his curiosity. He refuses to accept 'facts' at face value, he won't gloss over grey areas. He likes to see or experience a situation first hand before he comes to any conclusion, and he frequently interrogates apparent experts to test the wisdom of their knowledge. As a result, he always takes the shortest route to the information he needs, and invariably makes an informed and enlightened decision. As a bonus to himself, he increases his knowledge base en route.

How often have you heard someone say, "Oh, I presumed you knew that!", or "I assumed that had already been taken care of!", or "I just thought people would understand how to do that." Eager to reduce workloads, we so often skip a few steps to speed up a process, and find that we've only succeeded in creating roadblocks. Assumptions lead to frustrations, so:

- **Don't assume** that other people know what they're doing. Learn to challenge and accept challenges in return.
- **Never expect** that your sources will be objective. Go and see for yourself and then decide what to do.

- **Never imagine** you'll be right first time. Learn to pause and reflect before you take action.
- **Don't accept** seemingly authoritative facts and figures before checking them yourself.
- **Don't presume** that you need to continue doing things the way they've always been done. Do things differently.

Excellent Leaders do Their Homework

People don't tend to notice the effect of preparation until it's missing. Knowing this, choose to anticipate rather than assume, because anticipation promotes, encourages and facilitates better preparation. There will be times when you're caught unaware and you may be forced to wing it. That would certainly be better than drying up on the spot. However, try not to do it too often because it is likely to unsettle whoever's listening to you. Your approach may suggest that your audience is not worthy of your time, effort and concentration. If you are clearly winging it, people begin to wonder if you know what you're talking about and they start to question the extent of your authority. They ask themselves whether you are worth their attention, let alone their loyalty. If you wing it too often, you're wasting people's time.

The best leaders are skilled in the art of anticipation. They've learned to see round corners and are prepared for what comes next. There's no substitute for preparation, no matter how smart you are. It's hard work, and part of it will be wasted; the problem is that you will only know which part with hindsight. The better you anticipate what's required and prepare yourself with what's necessary, the less you'll find yourself needing to make assumptions.

- **Be prepared** to do your research and always allow time for rehearsal. Assimilate information and then communicate it well.
- **Keep your preparation** within realistic boundaries, to avoid the potential dangers of paralysis through analysis.
- **Learn to anticipate** the actions of those around you by getting to know how they feel, and how they function.
- **Be watchful** for opportunities as well as obstacles. Prime yourself to act, rather than react.
- **Raise your level** of awareness and education, so that you are equipped to meet your destiny.

Excellent Leaders Keep It Simple

I don't think that I have the ability to absorb any more acronyms. I have worked with people from many different industries, each one with its own secret shared language. I'm tired of trying to keep up with these obscure terms that are often only comprehensible to the people that coin them. It's true that, once you understand the terminology, once you are admitted to the club, you share a common purpose with fellow members. As the fellowship develops, your common language becomes more complex and exclusive. Members of the group seek to increase their self-importance and camouflage their lack of knowledge beneath the complexity of jargon.

True leaders strive continuously to simplify. Their quest is for clarity and they will make it their mission to translate, interpret, articulate, envision and describe until everybody shares an equal understanding and an overriding passion. Clear, compelling and credible messages provide the foundation for enlightened advancement and communal success. An organized mind, schedule and work methods will facilitate opportunities to be proactive. Consistent, instead of confused behaviour will engender trust and confidence.

- **Learn to understand** how other people need to hear the message
- **Stick to the basics** and be prepared to repeat them.
- **Act as interpreter** for the complex communicators within your enterprise.
- **A picture** is worth a thousand words. Learn to fill the canvas.
- **Articulate** your hopes, values and beliefs in words of one syllable.

Excellent Leaders Don't Wait to be Asked

Those that follow are searching for leaders; people who will take decisive action on their behalf. In return, the majority of leaders don't wait to be asked. They've already anticipated and understood the need, and they're ready to act. Proactivity is a vital element of leadership. Good leaders are proactive learners, who don't hesitate to act on strongly held beliefs, and have a habit of working energetically to overdeliver their promises.

- **Develop** your leadership skills through the experience of activity. Be prepared to learn from your mistakes.
- **Give more** than you've been asked for. People will thank you.
- **Cultivate** the energy to become the lead runner. You'll always be ahead of yourself.
- **He who hesitates** is lost. Go with your gut reaction.
- **Speak** on behalf of those who can't do it for themselves.

Recover Your Balance

We are living in a time when if you can balance three spinning plates on three sticks, you are rewarded with a fourth. And then a fifth

STEPHAN RECHTSCHAFFEN MD

—FOUNDER OF THE OMEGA INSTITUTE FOR HOLISTIC STUDIES

Have you ever noticed how the people that you most admire seem to do well at everything? They appear to have attained a sense of balance in the midst of the competitive demands of daily life. It's a skill that so often eludes us, but, with practice, it's one that we can all acquire. Balanced people take a holistic approach to their lives and their responsibilities. They see themselves as a sum of many different parts and aim for the synergy they can create by combining these multiple personalities effectively. It's often by finding their equilibrium that these individuals emerge as leaders.

At the end of my years, as I reflect on my life, I am certain that I will not wish I had spent more time at the office. There are few among us who make it our goal to spend more time working. A recent Ipsos-Reid poll suggests that balance is what many of us seek. Researchers asked 1,000 individuals to list their top indicator of personal career success. Work-life balance was the top selection of 30% of the poll. Linda Duxbury, a business professor at Carleton University, and a leading researcher on work-life issues suggests that "People feel that they can't have work success without life success. People want their job to be interesting, they want to make a difference, they want to be consulted, they want to learn."[45] Why then does work continue to absorb such an incredible amount of our time? Why are there still so many corporate cultures that encourage their employees to put their work before everything else, encroaching on family and leisure time with weekend travel schedules, midnight e-mails and a permanent atmosphere of crisis? The best and brightest leaders have learned to balance their priorities and proactively encourage the people who surround them to do the same.

- Your career can't run your life, because you are the one in charge of it. How much time do you devote to your work? Is your chosen career path aligned with your values, beliefs and life goals?
- When was the last time you visited your doctor for a check-up? Do you have time for regular exercise? Does your diet reflect a healthy lifestyle?

- How much thought do you put into the time spent with family and friends? Do you view your weekends as time to recover lost energy from the previous week? How much time do you spend planning interactions with the significant people in your life? Are you paying more attention to spreadsheets than memories?
- When was the last time you stopped to take care of the internal you? Great leaders nurture strongly held inner values and beliefs, and communicate their spirituality with intelligence and enthusiasm.
- How much money do you spend beautifying your outward appearance compared with your investment in the contents of the inner you? Leaders are lifelong learners, who feed their hunger from the inside out.

We all walk a daily tightrope. It's a balancing act. Our true progress depends on how well we maintain our equilibrium.

Leadership: Run That By Me Again

- **Study to be a leader**
  They are not born, but made. Start your apprenticeship

- **Eat quiche**
  Progressive leaders combine strength with humanity

- **Be of service**
  No one likes to be led

- **Make yourself unpopular**
  Leaders can't be everybody's friend

- **Shut up & listen**
  A clear communicator doesn't do all the talking

- **Set an example**
  Your attitude, behaviour & actions describe the surrounding culture

- **Pay attention to detail**
  From little acorns, mighty oak trees grow

- **Assume nothing**
  Sound familiar? It's worth repeating

- **Be prepared**
  The best leaders are skilled in the art of anticipation

- **Keep It Simple**
  True leaders simplify

- **Don't hesitate**
  Proactivity defines leadership

- **Recover your equilibrium**
  Balanced people don't fall down

7

Pay It Forward

"When a man dies they who survive him ask what property he has left behind. The angel who bends over the dying man asks what good deed he has sent before him."

THE KORAN

An Attitude of Gratitude

We're often so busy chasing the goal, that we forget to be grateful for the progress we've made in reaching it. There are times that we're simply too afraid to stop for a moment to recognize the abundance of life, for fear that we'll get left behind as the world hurtles past us at breakneck speed. In our hurry, we fail to acknowledge the sum of our experiences, good or bad, and the contribution they have made to our lives and our characters. Jewish oral tradition holds that man is born with his hands clenched, because on entering the world, he desires to grasp everything. It's true that, throughout much of our lives, our thoughts are focused on acquisition, with little regard for the means of possession or the selfless sacrifices that others have made as facilitators on our behalf. Gradually, as we grow, we begin to realize that the journey itself can be more significant and enlightening than the final destination. Along the way, the people we meet, the lessons we learn, the evolution we experience, and the personal insights we gain can prove to be far more enriching than the prize we initially sought. But, while we enter the world with a scarcity mind-set, grasping what we can for fear of losing it, our aim should be to leave this world with a feeling of abundance, our hands open, grateful that there is nothing we need to take away with us.

Fourteenth century German mystic, Meister Eckhart said that, "If the only prayer you ever say in your entire life is 'thank you', it will be enough." That is true on so many levels. Ungrateful people breed negativity. No one gets any pleasure from giving to an ungrateful person. When you show appreciation, the object of your attention blossoms and flourishes. As soon as we stop focusing on what's lacking in life, once we become truly aware of all that we have, we are free to show gratitude to ourselves and to everyone and everything that has contributed to our success.

> *I have walked the earth for thirty years and, out of gratitude, want to leave some souvenir*
>
> **VINCENT VAN GOGH—ARTIST**

Gratitude breeds happiness, and happiness propagates success, so thank yourself for who you are and for everything that has brought you to this moment. Thank anyone who has ever been of help to you, however small his or her assistance. It is the small acts of gratitude, performed with humility and consistency that count the most. However, if this is all getting a little too sentimental for you, and you'd prefer to be more cynical, consider the plainly-spoken, pragmatic words of seventeenth century French writer and moralist, François, Duc de la Rochefoucauld, who said, "Gratitude among friends is like credit among tradesmen: it keeps business up, and maintains commerce. And we pay not because it is just to discharge our debts, but that we might the more easily find lenders on another occasion."

Harbouring resentment is too much a killer of dreams and growth. Be grateful for what you have and be determined to use it for the benefit of others. Gratitude helps us to put the past in perspective, to live in the moment, and to define our future. It turns denial into acceptance, and we're all familiar with the importance of acceptance as a foundation for success. In the words of author physician, Christiane Northrup, "Feeling grateful or appreciative of someone or something in your life actually attracts more of the things that you appreciate and value into your life."

Pause every now and then to enjoy the journey you've started. Keep a journal of your thoughts, experiences, feelings and hopes; it will help you to understand what it is that you already have to be grateful for. Be aware of the amount of Effort, Energy & Enthusiasm that you put into all your activities. Tell yourself what it is that you have achieved today and how it has brought you closer to your goals. Identify what it is that you have you done today to make a difference. Measure your progress in whatever unit seems appropriate—money earned, weight lost, time saved, chapters written, battles won, habits cured, happiness shared. Be grateful for what you have achieved, and reward yourself for it. And remember that even the smallest advance represents progress.

Make Yourself a Mentor

*N*o person was ever honoured for what he received.
Honour has been the reward for what he gave

CALVIN COOLIDGE
—30TH PRESIDENT OF THE UNITED STATES

Forget about returning favours, and start focusing on passing goodwill to the next person in line. *Pay it Forward* is a book by Catherine Ryan Hyde, a movie starring Kevin Spacey, Helen Hunt and Haley Joel Osment and the inspiration for a philanthropic social movement that encourages students to become agents for change. When we focus on paying someone back for a kindness, we limit the effect of the goodwill to the people who are directly involved in the exchange. Paying a kindness forward, without any expectation of recompense, is all about building an infinite network of goodwill.

Picture yourself living your dream. You've put in the work, made the mistakes, endured the failures and developed the knowledge. You've achieved success and now it's your turn to help someone else achieve theirs. As a mentor, you can encourage your apprentice with knowledge, objectivity, feedback and perseverance. Don't limit yourself to work-related mentoring, because you can use your experience in any area of life to enhance someone else's skills and self-perception. Think of yourself as a guide, who will act as a catalyst, a resource, a facilitator, a networker and a problem solver. To do this you will need to listen, question and understand. You will need to advise rather than instruct.

Although wisdom is a valuable asset for mentoring, it's not essential to have crossed the dreaded threshold into middle age (or beyond) in order to be a powerful influence on someone else. There is nothing against peer-to-peer mentoring at any age. We are used to rapidly changing circumstances, and nowadays, personal advancement has more to do with merit than seniority. As a result, mentoring is more closely linked to experience than it is to time served. You could even find yourself involved in some reverse mentoring, using your knowledge to coach someone older than yourself; someone who just happens to be a novice in your area of expertise. There's also nothing to stop a mentee returning to mentor his master. Many apprentices, having rapidly absorbed and applied the wisdom of a mentor, will make significant advances in their field of expertise and will invariably be eager to share new knowledge and insights with their former advisors.

The mentoring relationship is not one that needs to be formally acknowledged (although structured mentoring programs are becoming increasingly popular). While many mentoring relationships can be long lasting, you could also succeed in mentoring someone as the result of a chance meeting, an impromptu response to a casual question, a common focus through a shared interest, or an unexpected introduction by a mutual friend. Many mentoring partnerships are a result of happenstance and evolve without either party making a conscious effort to prompt them. Today mentoring relationships may take place by e-mail, or over the phone, without either party ever laying eyes on the other. Biographies of famous historical figures can also make excellent mentors, in the absence of the real thing! It's also not unusual to come across instances of multiple mentoring, in the form of simultaneous webcasts or conference calls, (you'll find plenty of examples of this form of organized mentor communication on the websites of popular speakers). And you don't have to limit yourself to a single mentor relationship. Multiple mentors will help you gain a broader perspective and encourage diversity of thought.

There is evidence of mentoring in ancient African cultures, in Greek civilization, and in 18th Century France. It's not a novelty, it's a time-tested formula. The more you look, the more you'll find that behind every successful person there is a mentor; be it a parent, a sibling, a spouse, a friend, a teacher, a coach, an historical figurehead, a boss, a person of the cloth, a co-worker, or a celebrity. Anyone who has achieved success will acknowledge the benefit of mentoring and is, in turn, likely to become a mentor to someone else. Politicians and monarchs use mentoring to assure effective succession. Celebrities use mentoring to help overcome the stresses and pitfalls associated with a high profile. Artists use mentoring to promote the synergies of cross-fertilized ideas. Scientists use mentoring to speed up the pace of breakthrough discoveries.[46] Here are just a few examples of effective pairing:

In the Field of Entertainment
- Ingmar Bergman inspired Woody Allen
- Jack Lemmon gave shape to Kevin Spacey's focus
- Bing Crosby pointed Frank Sinatra in the right direction
- Madonna acted as guru for Gwyneth Paltrow
- Johnny Carson led us to Jay Leno

In Movies and on TV
- Jessica Tandy inspired Kathy Bates in **"Fried Green Tomatoes"**
- Michael Caine informed Julie Walters in **"Educating Rita"**
- Alec Guiness gave the force to Mark Hamill in **"Star Wars"**
- Ron Howard looked up to Henry Winkler in **"Happy Days"**

In Times Past
- Socrates played 'big brother' to Plato
- Ralph Waldo Emerson launched Henry David Thoreau
- Saul was David's inspiration
- Dr. Martin Luther King Jr.'s mission motivated Jesse Jackson

Leave a Legacy

We make a living by what we get. We make a life by what we give

SIR WINSTON CHURCHILL
—STATESMAN, POLITICIAN & LEADER

Material possessions are ephemeral. But our legacy, we hope, lives on long after we've departed this good earth. If you give greatly, you will live greatly, because you will find that you get back far more than you give. As they say, what goes around, comes around. Historically, the world's most successful people have been the greatest givers and their lives have been significantly enriched by their acts of generosity. If you don't hang on too tightly to what you have, you will make room for new experiences, new successes, new beginnings.

One of the most powerful reflective exercises that I have ever undertaken originated, I believe, from Stephen Covey. I suggest you try it. Take yourself off into a room that contains no distractions. Sit down in a chair, close your eyes for a moment, and imagine that you're attending your own funeral. What are people saying about you? How do they remember you? Does the person that you projected impress you? How did you score as a parent, a colleague, a partner, a sibling, a boss, a neighbour, a soul mate? What is *your* legacy? Avoid thinking purely in terms of finance or property. Expand your definition to include anything of value, tangible or spiritual, that you have been able to pass on to a future generation. If you're disappointed by what you see (and I certainly was), now is the time to start laying the foundations for your legacy. Because your legacy has its origins in the very moment that you make the decision to become instrumental in your own success.

The Beauty of Partnerships

We human beings are social beings. We come into the world as the result of others' actions. We survive here in dependence on others. Whether we like it or not, there is hardly a moment of our lives when we do not benefit from others' activities. For this reason, it is hardly surprising that most of our happiness arises in the context of our relationships with others

TENZIN GYATSO—THE 14TH DALAI LAMA

If you really want to add value to the legacy you are leaving, you will recognize that you cannot achieve anything of true substance alone. Unfortunately, many of us are products of an education system that has encouraged fierce competition. We have been persuaded to value the struggle for individual recognition and to be mistrustful of any attempts by others to combine resources. Teamwork has been a tough project for this generation and some of us have still to make the mental leap. However, in the current era of globalization, power no longer resides exclusively with the minority, in the means of production, or the items we produce. It no longer lies in the bricks and mortar of the buildings that house our corporations. Power lies in the minds of the people, and feeds on the information that they access, absorb, manipulate and use creatively every day. Creativity is a powerful resource in itself, but unhealthy competition can undermine creativity. If we strive to work together imaginatively and unselfishly, we will be helping to achieve each other's personal goals, and the combined legacy that we leave as a result will be brighter and more valuable than any of us could have achieved unilaterally.

The key to developing strong partnerships and forming effective teams, is good communication. Everything we do involves an approach or a response to someone else. Clear, careful and positive communication begins with an attitude of mind. Essentially the tone of your message is set long before you deliver it, and is the expression of your collection of paradigms; which is why it is so important to indulge in regular self-examination and ensure that your unique collection of paradigms is positive. Your intended message can also be affected by your choice of words; just think how e-mail can be used expertly as a highly effective communication tool, or disastrously as a deadly, and easily misinterpreted weapon. In the case of verbal communication, your tone of voice will add expression to your message and may convey anger, empathy, impatience, tolerance, excitement, or boredom. The more energetic, credible and sincere your message, the more enthusiastic you will find your reception. And, last, but by no means least, there's non-verbal communication to be considered. Incredibly, your body language says more about you than your tone of voice or choice of words combined. Your audience has already come to a number of conclusions about you before you ever open your mouth. Between 60% and 80% of a message is conveyed through body language, only 7%–10% through words,[47] and the rest is attributable to tone. The semaphore messages we send via our gestures explore extensive territory, from frowning to flirting. Blushing can suggest embarrassment, shyness, anger or shame. The Adam's apple jump can be an unconscious sign of emotional anxiety, embarrassment or stress. Throat clearing could indicate disagreement or deception, while arm folding could be either a defensive or an arrogant gesture. Spontaneous smiling can add a positive and unthreatening slant to anything. It's vitally important that we learn to convey the same message in both our verbal and unspoken communication. It is also important that we learn to understand the signals that other people send us:

- responsive
- reflective
- fugitive
- combative

Learn to pick partners who complement you. Assess your own strengths and weaknesses and gravitate towards people who will help you fill your own skill, knowledge and experience gaps. Move steadily towards people who believe in you, who share your values and applaud your dreams and determination. Associate with the kind of people you aspire to emulate. Just as birds of a feather flock together, winners congregate.

The 'Tenth' Rule

Some of the world's richest people have made it perfectly clear that the more they give, the more they get. We're talking about giving away money. J.L. Kraft, founder of the Kraft Cheese Corporation, who donated approximately 25% of his income to Christian causes said, "The only investment I ever made which has paid consistently increasing dividends is the money I have given to the Lord." J.D. Rockefeller, who was a scrupulous tither (he gave up 10% of his income to the common good), reportedly said, "I never would have been able to tithe the first million dollars I ever made if I had not tithed my first salary, which was $1.50 per week."[48] Oprah Winfrey is said to have made a habit of donating at least 10% of her spectacular annual income to charity throughout her adult life. Sir John Marks Templeton, founder of the successful Templeton Fund stated, "Tithing always gives the greatest return on your investment."[49]

The biblical practice of tithing is alive and well and living in your local community. The more you give it away, the more it multiplies. But your mindset has to be one of gratitude and abundance. If they have to pry it out of you, it ain't gonna work. Not everyone starts tithing by immediately giving away ten percent of income. Sometimes, it's a little less intimidating to start smaller, and work your way up to the target. Equally, there's nothing to stop you overstepping the 10% mark by expanding your generosity beyond the traditional boundaries.

But tithing doesn't have to be all about money. People who give freely of their time are in fact time tithers. Set aside some of your time to make a personal donation to your community.

You can donate your expertise by the hour for the benefit of others, without asking anything in return. It's all about leaving a footprint and making a difference. *Lifers* do time. Winners donate it. When you volunteer, you add value to the lives of the people who are your focus. And, although you ask for nothing in return, they will add value to yours.

Humility & Spirituality

*T**he sufficiency of my merit is to know that my merit is not sufficient***

ST. AUGUSTINE—BISHOP OF HIPPO

The 1952 children's classic by E.B. White, *Charlotte's Web*, has many lessons to teach us about loyalty, love, tolerance and the value of friendship. Rereading it recently with my daughter I was reminded of the resourcefulness of Charlotte, the grey spider, who is determined to save her doomed friend, Wilbur the pig. I was struck by the humility of both characters. It is a book that is full of unexpected and delightful wisdom. In a world that hadn't yet been introduced to the Internet, Charlotte the spin-doctor uses her web messages to save Wilbur from the butcher's knife and elevate him to stardom. Outside of Wilbur's friendship and admiration for her, the spider receives no credit for her part in the pig's success. Yet it is Charlotte who describes Wilbur as "not proud," and weaves the word HUMBLE into the center of her last web, for his benefit. Her friendship with Wilbur lends meaning to her own life.

And, in turn, Wilbur recognizes the place that she occupies in his heart long after her death, "It is not often that someone comes along who is a true friend and a good writer. Charlotte was both."

As good as you are, you haven't done your best work yet. And as good as your work gets, the credit for it will never be solely yours. As Winston Churchill said at the end of the Second World War, " I was not the lion, but it fell to me to give the lion's roar." Of humility, someone once said to me "The day you think you have it, is probably the day you need it most." You cannot wear humility with pride. Although I will leave it up to others to detect any traces of humility that I might possess, there are certainly a number of things that make me feel profoundly humble:

- Watching my children sleep
- Learning from their innocent wisdom
- Understanding that my wife is *naturally* kind and selfless
- Wishing that I didn't have to work so hard to be the same
- Stargazing

Stargazing never fails to remind me of our profound and ultimate insignificance in relation to the Universe. It reconnects me with my spirituality and my strong belief in a higher power; whoever, whatever, and wherever that may be. There's nothing comes close to the feeling you get when you stare up at the big night sky of the great outdoors, sprinkled with stars, and wonder who was responsible for this vastness. Cicero said that, "A man of courage is also full of faith." Those who believe in a higher order, are rewarded with serenity. They trust themselves, they trust others and they enjoy the comfort afforded by a strong spirituality. Those of us who desire to control every situation we encounter, will be left only with feelings of resentment. And resentment, in all its manifestations, could be the world's number one killer. Systemically, it attacks the very fabric of our fulfillment, our happiness and our self-esteem. We will never lead balanced lives while we cling to resentment. While we can both effect and affect, we are ultimately powerless to control relationships, circumstances and events completely. It is impossible to be in complete command of everything. In order to survive, we must learn that we are not ultimately in control. We must learn to let go of our resentment, try to keep our balance, and we must be willing to surrender to a power that is greater than ourselves. It is not even necessary to define or comprehend that power; we just need to be open to the presence of a higher order and willing to let go of the reins every once in a while. I do not presume to share your religious or spiritual beliefs, but I would encourage you to connect frequently with whatever higher power it is that you converse with, or answer to.

> *God give me the serenity to accept the things*
> *I cannot change, the courage to change the*
> *things I can and the wisdom to know the difference*
>
> **REINHOLD NIEBUHR**

Celebrate

> *To break crystal glasses*
> *In celebration,*
> *For you,*
> *When the dark crust is thrown off*
> *And you float all around*
> *Like a happened balloon*

ANNE SEXTON—POET

By now you're truly thankful, you've chosen an apprentice or two, you're working on your legacy, you've discovered the synergy of effective partnerships, you've shared the wealth, and you're suitably humbled by the whole experience. I guess it's time to throw a party! Whatever you do, please don't forget to celebrate. Honour your achievements, celebrate the milestones, the victories and the successes. Recognize the contribution of your partners and supporters; the people who have stayed the course with you and who have undoubtedly played a significant role in the achievement of your dream. Celebrate well, and celebrate frequently, for what's the point of realizing your dreams if they don't make you smile? If you forget to celebrate, you risk arriving at your destination without even realizing that you are there.

Celebrate all the little victories. Celebrate the contributions; not only yours, but those of everyone who played a part. Above all, celebrate the new journey that you are about to begin. What's your next step? Don't forget that it's time to recognize your new aspirations and to set yourself some new goals.

Pay It Forward: Run That By Me Again

- **Say thank you**
  If it's the only thing you do, it will be enough

- **Keep a journal**
  You'll begin to understand how much you've achieved

- **Find yourself an apprentice**
  Be the shortcut to someone else's success

- **Become a virtual mentor**
  You can help without being face to face

- **Attend your own funeral**
  What legacy will you leave?

- **Learn to give**
  If you give greatly, you will live greatly

- **Work with partners**
  You cannot achieve anything of true substance alone

- **Turn to tithing**
  The more you give, the more you get

- **Volunteer**
  Lifers do time. Winners donate it

- **Have some humility**
  As good as you are, you haven't done your best work yet

- **Throw a party**
  Celebrate your achievements and reward your supporters

- **Repeat as necessary**
  The more you win, the more you enjoy the rewards

The Last Words

*"If all economists were laid end to end,
they would not reach a conclusion."*
GEORGE BERNARD SHAW, ANGLO-IRISH PLAYWRIGHT

Learning Lessons

Typically, a book like this would wrap up with a clear conclusion of some sort. I hesitate, not because I'm an economist, but simply because there is no conclusion that will resonate equally with all of us. Each of you will come away with very different thoughts and feelings as a result of reading this book. It is likely that your opinions and resolutions will take a very different shape to my own. As far as possible, I'd like you to draw your own conclusions.

Putting this book together has helped me to focus. Truthfully, in its creation, I've been helping myself. In the exercise of trying to reach you, I have, in fact, come closer to me. In framing the 7 Step Approach, I have brought our shared imperatives into a more accessible part of my own consciousness. Also, in truth, it would be misleading of me to pretend that I always practise what I preach. That wouldn't be credible. For most of the time I am trying to achieve what I know I should and, if I'm honest, sometimes I'm not even doing that. However, knowing I've gone the extra mile by committing my thoughts to paper and publishing them is a good feeling... one of proactive contribution to my own progress. I've resolved to have the courage, the clarity and the discipline to go the extra mile more often.

Making a Difference

At the root of success are both conscious choice and commitment. They are preceded by a willingness to change. Successful people have made the choice to become winners instead of *lifers*. Winners leave a legacy. *Lifers* are simply here to mark time. In choosing to succeed, we take the most important step of our life. We release the potential energy that is stored within every one of us. By taking that step and making choices together in this book, hopefully we have minimized the associated fear and hesitation. Whatever kind of life change you're looking for, personal or professional, I hope you have come closer to it, or at least found the courage to seek it, within these pages.

There's no better time to choose to succeed. Now is the time to commit to a new future. If we're willing to do something different, we open the door to possibility, and progress will follow. With the right attitude and a clear vision of where we want to be, the path ahead will open up. We must cultivate the self-confidence to achieve our dreams and recognize the responsibility we have to make a difference in this world. We must refuse to be discouraged by the obstacles that appear throughout our journey, and be encouraged by the fact that they're here to strengthen us. If we face our difficulties and seek help in resolving them, we'll retain the focus of our objectives. And, as we gain strength through our successes, let us learn to leave a legacy through leadership.

The measure of our success as individuals, and as a society, is in the progress we have made, we make now, and the degree to which we will commit to that progress going forward. Let us celebrate the ability and the willingness we have to make choices and to take action. Let us celebrate the freedom we have and the permission we give ourselves to achieve our goals. Let us exercise an attitude of gratitude for the abundance in all our lives and "Feed The Good Dog" with a focus on the good and the positive. Strive for these moments of clarity.

Get up!

Get up!

Do something!

Make the choice to succeed!

7 Steps to Success

Step 1: Begin With An Attitude Of Mind

The pose you strike, the posture you assume, the perspective you choose, the opinions you express, the behaviour you model, and the temperament you display, all speak about the person you are. You get out of life exactly what you are prepared to invest in it. Energy and enthusiasm are contagious. Attitude is everything.

Step 2: Define Your Vision

When you feel that you have a reasonable understanding of where you are now, you can define where it is you want to go next, and start to create the map that's going to get you there. Identify your assets and your liabilities and set some goals.

Step 3: Have Confidence In Yourself

Encourage yourself to overcome your fear of failure, tell yourself that you're fully prepared to fail as many times as it takes to succeed, and you'll find that you stop worrying about what people think. Force yourself to take some risks.

Step 4:   Recognize Your Responsibility

Progress wants to happen. We've each been given something to add to this world that wasn't here before we arrived and it's time to answer the call. Embrace change, become accountable for your future and you'll start making progress. Remember, the simple difference between dreams and reality is action.

Step 5:   Deal With Difficulties

En route to success, you're going to face a series of obstacles. Don't try to walk round them. Face up to whatever is in your way, clear the path and continue with the journey. Prioritize your problems, hold on tight to your objective, and seek out people who can help you live your dream

Step 6:   Become A Progressive Leader

Like anything else, leadership can be learned. But people don't like to be led, so learn to serve. Winning-coach and motivator, Lou Holtz, was so right when he suggested that everything in life and everything in business is about helping other people get what they want.

Step 7:   Pay It Forward

Sometimes, the journey itself can be more significant and enlightening than the final destination. Master the simple art of saying thank you and learn to turn your gratitude into a legacy.

Sources of Influence

Personal Power II, Anthony Robbins, Robbins Research International Inc., 1996

How I Retired at 26!, Asha Tyson, ADT Publishing, 2002

You Were Born Rich, Bob Proctor, LifeSuccess Production

How to Win Friends & Influence People, Dale Carnegie, Pocket Books, Simon & Schuster, 1982

How to Stop Worrying and Start Living, Dale Carnegie, Pocket Books, Simon & Schuster, 1985

Living the Good Life, David Patchell-Evans, Stoddart, 2000

The Four Agreement, Don Miguel Ruiz, Amber-Allen, 1997

Manifest Your Destiny, Dr. Wayne W. Dyer, Harper Paperbacks, 1997

The Spirituality of Imperfection, Ernest Kurtz & Katherine Ketcham, Bantam, 1994

The Millionaire Mindset, Gerry Robert, Awesome Books, 1999

Dig Your Well Before You're Thirsty, Harvey Mackay, Doubleday, 1997

Golf My Way, Jack Nicklaus, with Tom Bowden, Simon & Schuster, 1974

Buck Up, Suck Up…and Come Back When You Foul Up, James Carville & Paul Begala, Simon & Schuster, 2002

The Learning Paradox, Jim Harris, Hignell, 1996

The Right Mountain: Lessons from Everest On The Real Meaning of Success, Jim Hayhurst, John Wiley & Sons, 1997

Beyond Negative Thinking, Joseph T. Martorano, M.D. & John P. Kildahl, Ph.d., Avon Books, 1989

Do Right & Do Right II, Lou Holtz

www.gripthis.com, Les Williams (Corporate Gardener),

The Road Less Traveled & Beyond, M. Scott Peck, M.D., Simon & Schuster, 1997

Shackleton's Way, Margot Morrell & Stephanie Capparell, Penguin Books, 2002

The One Minute Millionaire, Mark Victor Hansen, Robert G. Allen, Harmony Books, 2002

Tuesdays with Morrie, Mitch Albom, Doubleday, 1997

The Power of Positive Thinking, Norman Vincent Peale, Fawcett Columbine, 1996

Do What You Are. Discover the Perfect Career for You Through the Secrets of Personality Type, Paul D. Tieger & Barbara Barron-Tieger, Little Brown & Company, 1995

Leadership, Rudolph W. Giuliani, Hyperion, 2002

What To Say When You Talk To Yourself, Shad Helmstetter, Ph.D., Pocket Books, Simon & Schuster, 1987

Fish, Stephen C. Lundin, Ph.D., Harry Paul & John Christensen, Hyperion, 2000

Living the 7 Habits, Stephen R. Covey, Simon & Schuster, 1999

First Things First, Stephen R. Covey, A. Roger Merrill, Rebecca R. Merrill, Fireside Simon & Schuster, 1995

Return on Imagination, Tom Wujec/Sandra Muscat, Prentice Hall, 2002

Notes

1 www.fastcompany.com/online October 2000

2 *What To Say When You Talk To Your Self*, Shad Helmstetter, Ph.D. 1982, Pocket Books

3 www.smiles-video.com and The Seattle Times, No gloomy riders on Reggie Wilson's Metro bus, Christine Clarridge February 2, 2002

4 *First Things First*, Stephen R. Covey, A. Roger Merrill, Rebecca R. Merrill, Simon & Schuster 1994, Covey Leadership Center Inc.

5 Create an Abundant Life, Public Television broadcast, December 2002

6 *Elements of Success*, Leslie Fieger http://www.delfinworld.com/leslie_secrets/secrets5.htm

7 There is a question mark hanging over the authenticity of either university survey, with Yale alumni archives yielding no evidence of the study. Personally, I share the sentiments of goal guru Brian Tracy, who suggests that if the Yale story isn't true, it certainly should be! (Lawrence Tabak, Fast Company Issue 6 p.38, December 1996 http://www.fastcompany.com/online/06/edu.html)

8 www.inspirationalstories.com/5/537.html 18 Holes in His Mind by Author Unknown, A 2nd Helping of Chicken Soup for the Soul

9 *Golf My Way*, Jack Nicklaus with Tom Bowden, Simon & Schuster, 1974

10 *Imagine the Dream*, Joel Garfinkle, Dream Job Coaching, www.dreamjobcoach.com/imaginedreams.html

11 *Goal Setting*—Powerful Written Goals in 7 Easy Steps! Gene Donohue www.topachievement.com/goalsetting.html

12 Lou Holtz. *Do Right & Do Right II*

13 *Goal Setting—Powerful Written Goals in 7 Easy Steps!* Gene Donohue
www.topachievement.com/goalsetting.html

14 http://home.att.net/-rjnorton/Lincoln
http://showcase.netins.net/web/cretive/lincoln/speeches/falures.htm

15 Shad Helmstetter. *What to Say When You Talk to Yourself.* Pocket
Books, Simon & Schuster, 1987

16 *The Seven Principles for Making Marriage Work*, Dr. John M. Gottman,
Nan Silver, Three Rivers Press May 16, 2000

17 Les Brown: *It's Possible/*Don Miguel Ruiz: *The Four Agreements.* Amber
Allen Publishing 1997

18 Danny Hillis, keynote address at Siggraph 2001, Los Angeles, 12-17
August 2001, (Return on Imagination, Tom Wujec/Sandra Muscat ,
Prentice Hall 2002, Chap 2 p.32)

19 Les Brown. *It's Possible*

20 James Carville & Paul Begala. *Buck Up Suck Up… and Come Back
When You Foul Up.* Simon and Schuster 2002 p29

21 Sara Henderson.

22 Ray Bradbury

23 Allison DB, Fontaine KR, et al. Annual deaths attributable to obesity
in the United States. JAMA. 1999, 282(16): 1530-1538.

24 *Living the Good Life. Your Guide to Health and Success.* David Patchell-
Evans. Stoddart Publishing Co. Ltd 2000

25 *Software Strongman Bill Gates*, by David Gelernter
http://www.time.com/time/time100/builder/profile/gates.html

26 http://www.hhs.se/personal/suzuki/o-English/Austria.html

27 http://www.schulzmuseum.org/timeline.html
http://www.schulzmuseum.org/schulzbio.html

28 *Great Failures of the Extremely Successful*, Steve Young, Tallfellow Press 2002

29 http://www.census.gov.ipc/www/world.html
http://www.census.gov.ipc/www/idbsum.html

30 http://www.ship.edu/-cgboeree/maslow.html *Personality Theories.*
Abraham Maslow 1908–1970 Dr. George Boeree

31 http://www.freethechildren.org/info/whatisftc1a.htm

32 Doug Wead Audio Tapes. *Coming Back Stronger.*

33 Toy Story, Insider Spectrum, *Report on Business*, December 2002

34 *Return on Imagination. Realizing the Power of Ideas.* Tom Wujec/Sandra Muscat, Financial Times, Prentice Hall 2002

35 The Progressive Policy Institute
    http://www.ppionline.org/ppi_ci.cfm?knlgAreaID=107&subsecID=1
    23&contentID=926

36 Don Miguel Ruiz: *The Four Agreements.* Amber Allen Publishing 1997

37 Sir Ernest Shackleton, from his own book, South.

38 www.shackletonsway.com/homepage.htm

39 Shackleton's Way, Margot Morrell & Stephanie Capparell. Chapter 1, The Path to Leadership.

40 Shackleton's Antarctic Adventure (A Giant-Screen Film)
    http://main.wgbh.org/imax/shackleton/shacklton.html

41 Toxic Shock, Peter Frost, Globe Careers. The Globe and Mail, Wednesday, February 5, 2003

42 Colin Powell, *A Leadership Primer* PowerPoint Presentation

43 Leadership, Rudolph W. Giuliani, Hyperion 2002, pp. 46–50

44 http://www.theatlantic.com/politics/crime/windows.htm
    http://www.fightcrime.net/windows.htm

45 *The Globe And Mail*, Globe Careers, May 7, 2003. Katherine Harding

46 Mentors Peer Resources http://www.mentors.ca

47 http://www.bodylanguagetraining.com

48 W. A. Criswell, A Guidebook for Pastors, p. 154

49 *The One Minute Millionaire, The Enlightened Way to Wealth,* Mark Victor Hansen & Robert G. Allen, 2002 Harmony Books, New York, New York

FEED THE GOOD DOG

Is there someone you know who could benefit from reading **Feed the Good Dog**? It is the perfect gift for anyone looking for a way to help them 'reach higher' toward developing their true potential. After all, why keep a good thing to yourself?

To order: 1. Mail this form and cheque to ROSE LINE Publishing
                2. Phone toll-free: 1-800-282-0718
                3. On-line at **www.feedthegooddog.com**

Please send me _____ copies of **Feed the Good Dog** at $16.95 US/ $22.95 CDN each, plus $5 shipping and handling (Canadian residents please add GST and PST). I have enclosed a cheque made payable to "ROSE LINE Publishing" in the amount of $ _____

Name: _____

Address: _____

_____

City: _____ Province/State: _____

Postal Code/Zip: _____ Phone: _____

Mail to: ROSE LINE Publishing
            147 Briarwood Road
            Unionville, Ontario L3R 2X1 CANADA
Please allow 4–6 weeks for delivery

For orders of ten or more books, we offer an attractive discount, please call for details: 1-800-282-0718

For speaking engagements or seminars contact us at:
www.feedthegooddog.com